Elements in Construction Grammar
edited by
Thomas Hoffmann
Catholic University of Eichstätt-Ingolstadt
Alexander Bergs
Osnabrück University

SYNTACTIC VARIATION FROM INDIVIDUALS TO POPULATIONS

Language as a Complex System

Jonathan Dunn
University of Illinois Urbana-Champaign

Shaftesbury Road, Cambridge CB2 8EA, United Kingdom

One Liberty Plaza, 20th Floor, New York, NY 10006, USA

477 Williamstown Road, Port Melbourne, VIC 3207, Australia

314–321, 3rd Floor, Plot 3, Splendor Forum, Jasola District Centre, New Delhi – 110025, India

103 Penang Road, #05–06/07, Visioncrest Commercial, Singapore 238467

Cambridge University Press is part of Cambridge University Press & Assessment, a department of the University of Cambridge.

We share the University's mission to contribute to society through the pursuit of education, learning and research at the highest international levels of excellence.

www.cambridge.org
Information on this title: www.cambridge.org/9781009644358

DOI: 10.1017/9781009420280

When citing this work, please include a reference to the DOI 10.1017/9781009420280

First published 2025

A catalogue record for this publication is available from the British Library

ISBN 978-1-009-64435-8 Hardback
ISBN 978-1-009-42030-3 Paperback
ISSN 2753-2674 (online)
ISSN 2753-2666 (print)

Additional resources for this publication at www.cambridge.org/deeplearningquant

Syntactic Variation from Individuals to Populations

Language as a Complex System

Elements in Construction Grammar

DOI: 10.1017/9781009420280
First published online: December 2025

Jonathan Dunn
University of Illinois Urbana-Champaign

Author for correspondence: Jonathan Dunn, jedunn@illinois.edu

Abstract: This Element presents a computational theory of syntactic variation that brings together (i) models of individual differences across distinct speakers, (ii) models of dialectal differences across distinct populations, and (iii) models of register differences across distinct contexts. This computational theory is based in Construction Grammar (CxG) because its usage-based representations can capture differences in productivity across multiple levels of abstraction. Drawing on corpora representing over 300 local dialects across fourteen countries, this Element undertakes three data-driven case-studies to show how variation unfolds across the entire grammar. These case-studies are reproducible given supplementary material that accompanies the Element. Rather than focus on discrete variables in isolation, we view the grammar as a complex system. The essential advantage of this computational approach is scale: we can observe an entire grammar across many thousands of speakers representing dozens of local populations.

Keywords: syntactic variation, dialect, register, individual differences, computational sociolinguistics

ISBNs: 9781009644358 (HB), 9781009420303 (PB), 9781009420280 (OC)
ISSNs: 2753-2674 (online), 2753-2666 (print)

Contents

Additional resources for this publication at www.cambridge.org/deeplearningquant

1 Variation in a Complex System

The essential idea behind this work is that the grammar is a complex system, a network (Schneider, 2020). This means that individual constructions are connected to one another through INHERITANCE RELATIONS (with some constructions being more item-specific versions of others) and SIMILARITY RELATIONS (with some constructions carrying the same form or the same meaning as others). If the grammar is structured as a network, then we would hypothesize that grammatical variations spread through this network structure and thus that differences between dialects, between registers, and between individuals are best represented as differences between networks.

The case-studies in this Element examine variation across individuals (authorship) and geographic populations (dialect) and contexts of production (register). In all three cases, we will show that the amount of syntactic variation is remarkable so long as we possess sufficient means of observation. We will quantify the amount of variation by taking a classification approach which predicts underlying categories (like dialect membership) given the usage of constructions. Higher prediction accuracy indicates that there is more variation because a category which has more unique variants is easier to distinguish. Thus, we will first show that there is significant syntactic variation in each case by using constructional features to predict individuals, dialects, and registers.

We will then use similarity measures to construct networks that represent variation in the population. A similarity measure allows us to estimate, for instance, how grammatically distinct individuals from Chicago and Los Angeles and New York are from one another. While classifiers are supervised models, having access to training samples, similarity measures are unsupervised. The first question, for classifiers, is the magnitude of syntactic variation if we observe usage in many contexts all over the world all at once. The second question, for similarity measures, is the structure of syntactic variation and how the diffusion of variants takes place across a grammar which is a complex system. How pervasive is syntactic variation? How is it organized within the grammar? How is it organized within the larger population? These are the questions that we address at scale using computational methods.

Going back to the idea that syntactic variation is both robust and widespread, what exactly constitutes *sufficient means of observation* in this context? There are three necessary components: First, we must have a model of the grammar which includes both (i) constructions at different levels of abstraction as well as (ii) relations between those constructions. This Element thus depends on recent computational work in Construction Grammar (Dunn, 2024), without which we would not be able to observe the grammar as a complex system.

Second, we must have observations of language use that adequately represent the speech community as a complex network, rather than carry out dialectology within a single local region, like Northeastern vs Midwestern American English, we need to view the population itself as a global network with varying degrees of mutual exposure between local nodes. This Element thus depends on recent work in geographic corpora (Dunn, 2020) without which we would not be able to observe the full range of speakers of English around the world.

Third, because modeling variation within a complex system goes beyond the capabilities of even multivariate regression models, we must have high-dimensional and network-based models in order to adequately observe variation. Thus, this Element depends on more recent work in machine learning, relying on classifiers and unsupervised similarity measures and graph-based models. In practical terms, these three components combine to enable a comprehensive computational theory of syntactic variation that was not previously feasible: computational grammars applied to large digital corpora and analyzed using high-dimensional models.

Returning to the case-studies, once we have shown how substantial the amount of syntactic variation is, our main hypothesis is that the structure of that variation depends on the network structure of the grammar. For instance, processes of diffusion are expected to follow pathways that already exist in the form of relations between constructions. This hypothesis can be divided into three testable predictions: *First*, we expect that different parts of the network will contain more or less amounts of variation; for instance, not all parts of the grammar will have equally high classification accuracy. *Second*, we expect that the three kinds of variation will exist in different parts of the grammar; for instance, we expect that individual variation exists in more concrete constructions (more item-specific), while register variation is spread across all constructions. *Third*, we expect that, if processes of diffusion are concentrated on specific nodes of the grammar, observed similarity relationships will not be constant across the grammar. For instance, New Zealand English might be more similar to Australian English in phrasal verbs but at the same time more similar to British English in passive constructions. In other words, diffusion – and thus synchronic – similarity operates across the existing network structure of the grammar.

This first section introduces a conceptual framework for combining computational syntax with computational sociolinguistics. To ensure reproducibility, all input data, resources, and analysis are available in an open source repository.[1]

[1] https://doi.org/10.17605/OSF.IO/A57US.

1.1 Computational Syntax and Computational Sociolinguistics

This section briefly contextualizes this work within both computational syntax and computational sociolinguistics in order to understand why the increased scale that computational methods provide is important. Starting with computational syntax, a construction grammar is a network of form-meaning mappings at various levels of schematicity (Goldberg, 2006) which are built out of emerging ontologies of slot constraints (Croft, 2013). This grammar is a network composed of inheritance relationships and similarity relationships between pairs of constructions (Diessel, 2023). CxG is a usage-based approach to syntax: concrete and item-specific constructions are learned first and only later generalized into schematic constructions (Doumen, Beuls, & Van Eecke, 2023; Nevens et al., 2022).

Given that the grammar is a complex system, variation will be influenced by three factors: first, the LEVEL OF ABSTRACTION or how schematic a construction is; second, the DEGREE OF CENTRALITY or how core a construction is within the grammar (Hollmann & Siewierska, 2011); and, third, the ORDER OF EMERGENCE or how early a construction is learned (Dunn, 2022). Because the indexicality or social meaning of constructions is a means by which they can be differentiated (Leclercq & Morin, 2023), variation is an inherent property of the grammar from the very beginning.

The basic idea in this Element is that we first use computational syntax to learn an unsupervised representation of the grammar of English and then use this rich feature space as a means of understanding variation across individuals, populations, and registers. Relying on unsupervised computational syntax means that (i) the methods are reproducible and do not begin with annotator bias; (ii) the grammar represents both inner-circle and outer-circle dialects equally, unlike annotated corpora; (iii) the grammar provides a much broader and deeper feature space for observing variation; and (iv) the structure of the grammar as a complex network is directly available to our experiments.

This work thus builds on a long history of computational models of the emergence of construction grammars, from specific families like argument structure constructions (Alishahi & Stevenson, 2008; Barak & Goldberg, 2017) to shallow but wide-coverage models of holophrase constructions (Wible & Tsao, 2010, 2020) to template-based methods that build on annotations and introspection (Perek & Patten, 2019). Some work has taken an agent-based approach in which individual learners acquire constructions during communication until all observed utterances can be successfully interpreted (Beuls & Van Eecke, 2023). This body of work as a whole can be viewed as a discovery-device grammar (Goldsmith, 2015) which formulates syntactic representations given exposure to a corpus. Thus, CxG as a theory can be viewed as a mapping between exposure and an emergent grammar.

At the same time, this work also builds on a long history of corpus-based models in computational sociolinguistics, in which an unelicited corpus of usage is taken as a representation of dialectal production (Grieve, 2016; Szmrecsanyi, 2013). This tradition depends on corpora that represent specific dialect communities, whether compiled manually (Greenbaum, 1996) or drawn from web pages (Cook & Brinton, 2017; Davies & Fuchs, 2015) or pulled from geo-referenced social media posts (Donoso, Sánchez, & Sanchez, 2017; Eisenstein, O'Connor, Smith, & Xing, 2014; Gonçalves & Sánchez, 2014; Mocanu et al., 2013; Wieling, Nerbonne, & Baayen, 2011).

Work in computational sociolinguistics has established that lexical usage on social media mirrors usage as captured by dialect surveys (Grieve et al., 2019) and also that digital communities develop their own nongeographic variants (Lucy & Bamman, 2021). Because corpora provide more samples, thus providing more robust and diverse examples of usage, computational sociolinguistics has also found that categories like gender are more complex when viewed at scale (Bamman, Eisenstein, & Schnoebelen, 2014). Other work has looked at the disproportionate influence that inner-circle varieties like American English exert in digital spaces (Gonçalves et al., 2018) and at how deeper syntactic variation can be modeled as differences in constraint rankings (Grafmiller & Szmrecsanyi, 2018; Szmrecsanyi & Grafmiller, 2023).

Much of this work has focused on variation across groups, with groups represented by categorical variables like gender or location or context. But the speech community is also a network in which each individual is a node represented by its degree of contact within the network (Fagyal et al., 2010). English, in particular, forms a global network with exposure and contact between geographically distant dialects. These long-distance connections are created as a result of immigration, mass media, and digital communication platforms (c.f., Dąbrowska, 2021). Thus, each local population is a node in a global network of English users. We must take seriously the idea that both language (Beckner et al., 2009) and the speech community (Schneider, 2020) are complex networks.

The advantage of a computational approach is scale: we can observe variation across a wider selection of the grammar and across a wider selection of the speech community. Traditional work has always been severely limited in scale, and as a result has placed undue importance on distinctions like weak vs strong ties. In part, this is because the networks being observed in such studies are cognitively and socially unrealistic (Fagyal et al., 2010). Such traditional work has also assumed that only face-to-face conversations are interactive

(Trudgill, 2014), much like early work in dialectology assumed that speakers were geographically immobile. Both of these assumptions, if they ever were valid, are clearly no longer applicable: the speech community now is highly mobile both within and between countries and engages in long-distance interactions through digital avenues like social media. Work in computational sociolinguistics has shown, for instance, that studies which rely on unrealistically small networks overstate the importance of strong vs weak ties within a network (Laitinen & Fatemi, 2022; Laitinen, Fatemi, & Lundberg, 2020).

This Element relies on social media data to observe individual and dialectal variation, but then considers variation across contexts in the final section. While traditional methods have relied on the idea of a pure vernacular as the only valid source of observing variation, this assumption is not suitable to language use in the contemporary world. Written and digital registers are important sources of exposure, and there is not a clear distinction between formal writing and the spoken vernacular. Even within a single register there are many sub-registers that can be difficult to distinguish: register is a continuum (Biber, Egbert, & Keller, 2020; Egbert, Biber, & Davies, 2015). Rather than ignore register variation in the quest for a pure vernacular, we therefore end this Element by looking at variation across contexts and explicitly compare the way in which dialectal variation and contextual variation are structured in grammar.

To conclude, this work is situated within the traditions of both computational syntax and computational sociolinguistics. Both rely on computational models and large corpora to expand the scale of our understanding of language and to make our findings more reproducible. This is important because, if both language and the speech community are complex networks, then variation can be seen as an emergent property of language use. Small-scale approaches which rely on manual analysis of only a few samples from a few speakers will always be inadequate for understanding a complex system. The Element shows in detail how we can move beyond these methodological limitations.

1.2 A Computational Model of the Grammar

A model of grammatical variation must operate on some feature space which serves as a description of the grammar itself. In early corpus-based work on syntactic variation, this description was simply a single alternation: for example, contracted vs noncontracted forms (Grieve, 2011), agreement in existential-*there* constructions (Collins, 2012), adverb placement in verb phrases (Grieve, 2012), or genitive and dative alternations (Szmrecsanyi et al., 2016). The problem is that studies of individual alternations have no capacity to generalize: Are other features undergoing the same direction of change? Do these features have an impact on other portions of the grammar, leading to syntactic chain-shifts? How representative are these features of the grammar as a whole? Is this variation located in the center or in the periphery of the grammar? These questions cannot be addressed given individual features.

As a result, the next wave of work focused on aggregating across individual features: for example, a set of 57 surface-level variants like nonstandard reflexives (Szmrecsanyi, 2013), a set of 135 surface-level variants like *previous* vs *prior* (Grieve, 2016), and a set of 3 more abstract constructions like the dative and the genitive (Szmrecsanyi & Grafmiller, 2023). While this line of work is less arbitrary than individual features, it is still based on fixed introspection-based choices derived from prestigious inner-circle varieties. More importantly, many of these representations remain relatively surface-level, often more on the lexical end of lexico-grammatical continuum. Given that the grammar ranges from highly item-specific holophrase constructions to highly abstract families of constructions like the transitive, where is variation located across levels of abstraction? We could never answer this kind of question using hand-curated surface-level alternations which are ultimately located in a single region of the grammar.

To resolve these weaknesses, more computationally-driven work has connected the study of variation within a grammatical feature space (Dunn, 2018a, 2019b) with grammar induction or the learning of such a feature space (Dunn, 2017). The idea in this approach is to view the feature space as a discovery-device grammar, *D*, which provides a usage-based model of how constructions emerge given exposure (a corpus, *CORPUS*). Thus, a specific grammatical feature space is the output of a discovery-device grammar: $G = D(CORPUS)$. As a result, the feature space is not fixed and need not implicitly maintain an inner-circle focus. A model of variation (*VAR*) works on top of a grammatical feature space: $VAR(G)$. Here that feature space is actually a model of an entire grammar and maintains its network structure: $VAR(D(CORPUS))$. So the grammar is a network learned from a corpus, its linguistic experience, and the model of variation operates on top of that replicable and dynamic feature space.

We have several important questions about language variation and change which can only be investigated using this high-dimensional discovery-device approach: *First*, do processes like diffusion operate on individual constructions alone or do they operate on nodes within the grammar, creating a pressure that applies with diminishing force as it passes through the grammar network? *Second*, can a dialect be influenced simultaneously in two different directions, so that individual constructions would show opposing directions of change? *Third*, what impacts does change in one part of the grammar have on other parts of the grammar, not because of continued diffusion but because of internal impacts from syntactic chain-shifts? *Fourth*, does the level of abstraction impact the order of variation, with more concrete and idiomatic and item-specific constructions changing first? These are all questions which we can only approach with a principled and systematic grammar: individual constructions or arbitrary collections of alternations are both inadequate to the task.

For these reasons, we need to start our study of grammatical variation with a reasonably adequate model of the grammar. We draw on work in computational construction grammar (Dunn, 2024). Constructions are constraint-based representations composed of (i) slots and (ii) slot-fillers that are derived from specific ontologies or systems of categorization. For example, in (1a) the construction has three slots or positions. The first slot is defined with semantic information and the remaining slots are defined with syntactic information. In this case, then, we have three positions and two ontologies or systems of categorization used to define what linguistic material those positions can hold. This is the basic form of a construction.

(1a) [TRANSFER-EVENT – NOUN PHRASE – NOUN PHRASE]
(1b) "send me the bill"
(1c) [*give* – NOUN PHRASE – *a hand*]
(1d) "give me a hand"

Small changes in these constraints can lead to significant changes in the set of utterances which they license. For example, if we replace the semantic slot-constraint in (1a) with a lexical constraint in (1c), we now have an item-specific and idiomatic construction, as in (1d). This construction is still productive in the sense that it licenses or produces a varied set of utterances; however, it is less productive and more concrete than the original in (1a). From a usage-based perspective, the grammar is learned from exposure to usage together with general learning principles. We would expect, then, that each individual has a unique set of linguistic experiences (different exposure) and would learn slightly different slot-constraints. Because constructions can overlap (e.g., 1a and 1c would produce some of the same utterances), individuals might have different sets of constructions even when their production largely overlaps.

The advantage of a discovery-device or computational approach to grammatical representation is that we can capture such differences. There is no theoretical reason to posit that all dialects of English have the same set of ditransitive constructions, for instance, or that each dialect has the same ontology of slot-constraints. A reliance on simplified, abstracted, bleached constructions is a practical problem: in our view, linguists in an armchair cannot use introspection to find out what the ontology of slot-constraints in Nigerian

English is or what the inventory of ditransitives in Indian English is. These are empirical questions. Our approach here is to model the learning of constructions given exposure, where *learning* is grammar induction using machine learning and *exposure* is a corpus. This is not an exact analogy to human learning; for example, language use in a corpus is structured much differently than language use in an embodied, situated context. It remains the case, however, that a corpus-based approach with a discovery-device grammar is much more realistic than previous methods based on individual constructions or arbitrary surface-level alternations.

The challenge of learning construction grammars and what that looks like computationally is a matter for other work (Dunn, 2017, 2018b, 2018c, 2019a, 2022, 2023a, 2024; Dunn & Nini, 2021; Dunn & Tayyar Madabushi, 2021). What we will do here is briefly sketch what such a grammar looks like:

First, a construction grammar must define the sets of slot-constraints. This encompasses both what ontologies are relevant (i.e., syntactic, semantic, etc) as well as which specific categories are actually in these ontologies. In computational CxG, this is done using distributed representations (i.e., embeddings).

Second, a construction grammar must define how such slot-constraints are combined into constructions. In computational CxG, this is a sequential model much like a phrase structure grammar (as opposed to, for instance, a relational model like a dependency grammar): slot-constraints are contiguous.

Third, a construction grammar must define how individual constructions are related to one another (i.e., parent-child relationships). In computational CxG, similarity between constructions is measured using both (i) similarity of representations and (ii) similarity of utterances in a reference corpus. These similarities are used to organize constructions at three levels of abstraction: first- and second-order constructions (the most concerete), third-order constructions (mid-level), and fourth-order constructions (the most abstract). In terms of hierarchy, fourth-order constructions are the parents of third-order constructions. These are learned upwards, starting from concrete surface-level forms. Thus, our exploration of syntactic variation here is organized by increasingly abstract constructions; first-order constructions have a single representation while fourth-order constructions are groups or families of related representations.

Fourth, a construction grammar must posit a means by which constructions are learned from exposure; in computational CxG the optimization metric is based on Minimum Description Length (Grünwald, 2007), which means that the learner is balancing what information needs to be memorized (tending towards large shallow grammars) and what information needs to be computed (tending toward small but highly abstract grammars). This balance implicitly depends on the amount of exposure: larger corpora, which encompass more linguistic experience, support larger and more item-specific grammars.

For the sake of example, we discuss several constructions from the tweet-specific grammar used in the Element. These examples are all first-order constructions; third-order and fourth-order constructions are more abstract families that combine these lower-level constructions. In (2) we see a noun phrase derived from the early-stage (local only) grammar (c.f., Section 1.3); there are two slots, each defined by a syntactic constraint. These constraints are in fact learned as centroids within an embedding space. The label SYN refers to the ontology used to define the slot constraint; the number 174 is an arbitrary identifier; the name <buttercream-custard> is a human-readable label which provides two exemplars of the category. As we might expect, this is not a generic notion of noun; here all fillers are edible physical items, such as *peanut butter cup*. In (3) we see a different noun phrase from the late-stage (multiple constraint) grammar; these slot-constraints are derived from three sources (lexical, syntactic, and semantic). These particular constraints result in definite noun phrases describing an individual, like *the happiest person*. These two noun phrases are simple examples of the range of utterances produced by simple data-driven slot-constraints.

(2) [SYN:174 <buttercream-custard> – SYN:174 <buttercream-custard>]
(2a) peanut butter cup
(2b) chocolate milk
(2c) banana ice-cream
(2d) chocolate fudge

(3) [SEM:141 <which-whereas> – SYN:66 <shadiest-silliest> – LEX: "person"]
(3a) the worst person
(3b) the smartest person
(3c) the funniest person
(3d) the happiest person

Comparable examples of verbal constructions are shown in (4) and (5). In (4), we see an early stage (i.e., with only syntactic constraints) construction with verbs of thinking that introduce a subordinate clause that is not included in the construction. For example, with *still don't know who* the construction contains the verb and adverb with an object relative clause attached, but not contained. In (5) we see a late-stage construction, here with only semantic constraints, that again contains a main clause verb phrase together with the subject of a subordinate clause, as in *i know i'm*. Because constructions are joined together to create a complete utterance, this would be combined with a construction covering the remainder of the subordinate clause with the overlapping slot-constraint providing the link in that chain.

(4) [SYN:100<always> – SYN:143<won't> – SYN:88<understand> – SYN:100<always>]
(4a) still don't know who
(4b) really do think that
(4c) just don't care if
(4d) honestly don't think he

(5) [SEM:1<he-we> – SEM:377<think-know> – SEM:1<he-we> – SEM:675<now>]
(5a) i know i'm
(5b) i think i'm
(5c) i swear i'm
(5d) i suggest that we

This section has described the grammatical representations and given a few examples of nominal and verbal constructions. For more discussion of the idea (i) of slot-constraints formulated as centroids within an embedding space, (ii) of early vs late grammars based on the order of emergence, (iii) of how constructions might be joined together into larger structures, and (iv) of how slot-constraints emerge, see an overview of computational CxG (Dunn, 2024).

1.3 Networks: Structure within the Grammar

Our reason for looking at variation across the grammar, rather than variation across a few constructions, is to understand how changes spread across the network and how syntactic chain-shifts can occur as these changes spread. The question in this section is how we move from viewing the grammar as a flat feature set – a set of constructions – to viewing the grammar as a connected network. We can categorize constructions based on (i) when they are learned or their order of emergence and (ii) their level of abstractness and (iii) their centrality in the grammar. In the first case we can contrast early and late constructions (order of emergence). In the second case we can contrast abstract vs item-specific constructions (level of abstraction). And in the third case we can contrast central and peripheral constructions (degree of centrality).

This approach to categorizing constructions within the grammar is visualized in Figure 1. The grammar as a whole contains 15,172 constructions

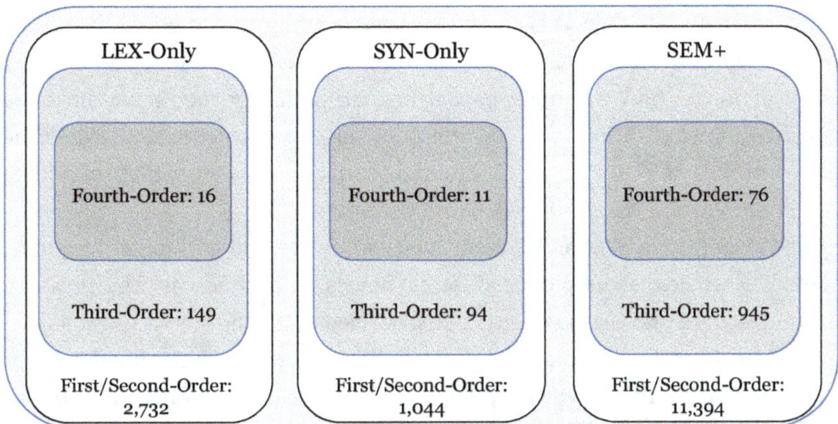

Figure 1 Division of constructions in the grammar by emergence and abstractness.

across orders of emergence and levels of abstraction. These are organized into 1,190 mid-level constructions (e.g., third-order) and 103 high-level (e.g., fourth-order) constructions. To be clear, a third-order construction is a bundle of related first-order constructions; thus, in terms of the inheritance hierarchy, the first-order constructions are children of a third-order construction and siblings of other first-order constructions in the same cluster. Rather than develop more abstract human-readable representations for third-order constructions, we instead look at many different first-order constructions as a way of understanding that more abstract representation.

We can examine differences by order of emergence by comparing groups from left to right in Figure 1. We can examine differences by level of abstraction by comparing nested boxes from top to bottom in Figure 1. And we can examine variation within specific nodes of the grammar by focusing only on siblings: members of the same box in Figure 1. Thus, considering the late-stage SEM+ grammar, we could observe 11,394 surface-level constructions or 945 mid-level constructions or 76 high-level constructions. These represent the grammar across different levels of abstraction. Finally, we can examine strata of centrality by using frequency weights derived from an independent reference corpus.[2]

What does this mean in theoretical terms? We might expect that individual differences within a given population occur in more concrete constructions (first-order) and at later stages of emergence (SEM+). We might expect that

[2] We operationalize *central* constructions to be more than one standard deviation above the mean frequency and *peripheral* constructions to be below the mean frequency.

similarity between dialects is consistent across sibling constructions but differs only in disconnected nodes of the grammar (i.e., within separate fourth-order constructions). And we might expect that different registers have the same constructions but differ in the centrality of those constructions. Dividing the grammar like this allows us to examine variation in a way that individual constructions or a flat set of constructions cannot.

The examples in Section 1.2 contrasted early-stage and late-stage grammars. Here we consider examples at different levels of abstraction. The previous examples were first-order constructions, defined as having slot-constraints that are drawn from the basic ontology (lexical items) rather than allowing other constructions as fillers. Here we look at examples of third-order and fourth-order constructions which are more abstract representations that contain many sibling constructions. These are only identified by cluster id, without a human-readable representation, so we examine each by giving three representative first-order constructions. But it is important to note that these constructions are more abstract than these first-order examples because they describe many such first-order siblings.

The three verbal constructions in (6–8) are siblings within a third-order construction. This means that they are more concrete individual constructions which correspond to the same abstract construction. When we examine variation, we could look at the lower-level frequencies of (6–8) individually or we could look at the higher-level frequencies of this third-order construction. This is what we mean by operating across different levels of abstraction. Here, each first-order construction has a main verb that encodes the subject's modal state while carrying out an action which is encoded within an infinitive clause.

(6) [SYN:185 <permitted> – SEM:14 <then-once> – SYN:67 <antagonize-placate>]
(6a) tried to intimidate
(6b) refused to allow
(6c) trying to spoil
(6d) unable to vanquish

(7) [SYN:185 <permitted> – SEM:14 <then-once> – LEX: *stop*]
(7a) failed to stop
(7b) trying to stop
(7c) able to stop
(7d) decided to stop

(8) [SYN:185 <permitted> – SEM:14 <then-once> – SYN:88 <understand-believe>]
(8a) delighted to see
(8b) refusing to forgive
(8c) obligated to love
(8d) seeks to reassure

At a higher level of abstraction, a fourth-order construction is similarly composed of many third-order constructions, thus encompassing a greater portion of the grammar. The constructions in (9–11) are first-order constructions which are examples of other third-order constructions within the same fourth-order construction represented in (6–8). In other words, (6–8) are siblings of one another and cousins of (9–11). The construction in (9) again uses the main verb to encode the subject's mental state, but now this is directed towards an adpositional phrase which is attached to but not contained within the construction. In (10) there is an infinitive verb which instead encodes the speaker's state, and in (11), more similar to (6–8), the object of the action is now included within the construction. These are three examples from other third-order constructions, all contained within the same abstract fourth-order construction. From the perspective of variation, we could observe differences at any of these levels of abstraction. From a usage-based perspective, we would expect more variation at lower levels of abstraction.

(9) [SYN:159 <terrified> – SEM:14 <then-once> – SEM:141 <which-whereas>]
(9a) excited over the
(9b) impressed at the
(9c) amazed when the
(9d) disgusted at the

(10) [SEM:14 <then-once> – SYN:168 <demonstrate> – SEM:141 <which>]
(10a) to applaud the
(10b) to recognize the
(10c) to welcome the
(10d) to embrace the

(11) [SYN:185<permitted> – SEM:14<then-once> – SYN:88<believe> – SEM:25<them>]
(11a) trying to convince me
(11b) fails to remind me
(11c) proceeded to ask us
(11d) supposed to tell me

These examples are all first-order constructions. Higher-order abstractions are made by viewing these more concrete constructions as children of larger and more diverse constructions. The emergence of constructions proceeds upwards, starting with first-order constructions and generalizing to higher-orders of structure.

1.4 Overlap: Comparing Grammar and Usage

We now have a robust network representation of the grammar that we can use for finding variation between individuals, populations, and registers. How do we conceptualize *differences* in the grammar? The main concept is OVERLAP: two individuals, for instance, will share a large portion of the grammar but will not share certain nodes within it. The more the two grammar networks overlap, the more similar these two individuals are.

We could calculate overlap in terms of the grammar itself (c.f., Dunn & Nini, 2021; Dunn & Tayyar Madabushi, 2021): if we learn a unique grammar given a simulation of the exposure experienced by an individual speaker of a dialect, for instance, how much does that learned grammar differ from the same simulation in other dialect areas? This is a comparison of the grammar itself because we have two networks learned independently under different conditions, where each *condition* is a type of exposure (i.e., a model of Midwest American English is exposed to corpora from that region).

Another approach is to calculate overlap in terms of the usage of a single umbrella grammar by different populations (c.f., Dunn, 2019b, 2023b): here we learn a single grammar network given a sample of usage from many dialects and individuals, essentially creating an abstraction which is not situated within a single speech community. We then compare dialect groups, for instance, given their usage of different portions of this grammar; some portions might be completely unused (and thus not entrenched at all), while other portions are used infrequently (and thus only weakly entrenched). Thus, dialects would differ in their relative entrenchment of different portions of the grammar.

These contrasting paradigms have their own strengths and weaknesses. Comparing grammars allows us to simulate different types of exposure and is more naturalistic in the sense that speakers of a dialect have arrived at that dialect directly rather than first learning a generic grammar and then selecting certain variants. On the other hand, comparing grammars in this way provides two distinct feature spaces which makes measuring overlap more difficult; and the grammar learning process itself is subject to certain bits of random noise so that some variation will be arbitrary.

Comparing usage allows us to obtain fine-grained measures of overlap within a single feature space and it maps well to noncomputational work in variation, which by definition assumes a single shared feature space through which each group is analyzed. On the other hand, the usage approach is not naturalistic because no individual learner has equal exposure to all dialects or attaches equal prestige to all sources of exposure. Thus, it is an artificial simulation of variation, albeit one whose artifice is shared by much previous work.

In this Element we compare usage. Thus, the methodology is to first learn a grammar network for each register (c.f., Section 1.2), in which all dialects and all individuals are equally represented. This forms an umbrella grammar which should capture portions of the grammar that, in fact, are acquired by only limited sections of the overall population. In other words, while our purpose is to study variation, we start with a grammar which essentially posits a single network for English within each register. We then take the usage of constructions as a measure of the entrenchment of different portions of this grammar within each population or individual.

Once we have learned this register-specific umbrella grammar, we use the token frequency of its constructions to estimate the entrenchment of each construction for individuals and populations. Higher token frequencies reflect entrenched forms. From a conceptual level, this methodology maps well onto previous work in dialectology; an exploration of grammar overlap situated within the learning process remains a question for future work.

1.5 Modeling Variation: Classification and Similarity

Given a grammar and a corpus of usage, our next challenge is to model variation in the entrenchment of that grammar for the group which produced that corpus. There are two basic approaches to this problem: classification (more common in computational work) and similarity measures (more common in dialectometry). Here we draw on both types of model and it is worth thinking through the essential differences between these models of grammatical variation.

The idea behind a classification approach is that we have multiple groups which we hypothesize will differ in the entrenchment of constructions: different dialects, for instance. The classifier takes these group labels as a given, never directly evaluating their validity. The classifier is instead focused on finding parts of the grammar that can reliably distinguish between the given groups: what is the difference between American English and British English grammar, for example, such that we can reliably predict for any given sample whether it belongs to one or the other dialect? Variation is ultimately about linguistic differences between groups and classifiers are the most robust computational model available for finding and characterizing differences.

There are two main advantages to a classification approach: *First*, classifiers can work in high-dimensional feature spaces and are not troubled by overlapping or correlated features (which many constructions are by definition). *Second*, classifiers come with a ground-truth evaluation: how accurately can they predict dialect membership? At the end of the modeling process, we can measure precisely how well the classifier works and we can evaluate the relative magnitude of variation in different parts of the grammar.

But there are some disadvantages to a classification approach as well: *First*, the groups must be defined in advance and there is no direct mechanism for saying that a sample is partly British English and partly American English. We can use a classifier to simulate similarity values and we can conduct an analysis of errors; but no sample on its own can straddle the category boundary. *Second*, a classifier requires training data that takes the form of samples from the corpus together with their label. Actual variation emerges from the kinds of exposure a learner encounters. It is not the case that a human first has equal exposure to all dialects and then acquires their own dialect by selection. Thus, while quite powerful as a model of variation a classifier is somewhat unnatural in that it is exposed to both samples and labels. On the other hand, this difference is perhaps not so strong because human learners, also, can guess the group memberships of their interlocutors. This is especially the case if dialect perception is indeed robust, so that speakers can intuit the dialects they are exposed to. At any rate, it is the supervised nature of classifiers that makes them both a powerful but also somewhat unnatural model of variation.

An alternate approach is to calculate pairwise similarity values between individual samples, so that labels like American English are not included in the model. This is an unsupervised approach, not trained with examples but allowing variation to emerge naturally as the difference between pairs of samples. Similarity measures are pairwise: for instance, between one sample of American English from Chicago and one sample of British English from London. By sampling many pairs from the underlying population we can construct confidence intervals on the similarity between the grammar of these dialects themselves.

The scale of similarity estimates, however, makes them difficult to interpret on their own. For instance, in this Element we work with 304 local populations distributed across fourteen countries. This creates a tremendous number of pairwise similarities between local dialects (46,360 to be precise). We thus make sense of these similarities by creating a graph structure in which each local dialect is a node and the similarity between them within some part of the grammar is the edge weight.

The advantage of a similarity-based approach is that we make no assumptions about labels: the ontology of dialects is discovered, not assumed. For example, we conduct an accuracy-based validation of all similarity measures used in this Element which checks to see if samples from the same condition (i.e., the same individual or the same dialect) or more similar to one another than to samples from another condition. Thus, this validation step ensures that each individual or dialect or register does, in fact, have a unique grammar. Further, we can measure homogeneity and heterogeneity within dialects more directly because individual samples can be placed between categories. Thus, we could see that one local region is situated halfway between two standard national dialects like American and British English. This is the reason that dialectometry has often relied on similarity values.

But there are a few disadvantages as well. In the first case, an unsupervised approach views all features as equal contributors to similarity; this means that the signal of variation can be overwhelmed by the noise of unvarying parts of the grammar. Put another way, a classifier can pick a varying construction out of a haystack, but a similarity measure will be prone to overlooking small differences. The larger the feature space, the more true this becomes. In the second case, similarity measures do not have a direct ground-truth evaluation unless we happen to have participant-based ratings of dialect similarity, which are themselves not a direct view of differences in dialect production. And yet it is essential that we have some measure for how good the model is. Thus, the most common approach is to evaluate similarity measures using a classification task: for instance, what percentage of samples of American English are most similar to other samples of American English? The important point is that even unsupervised models must be evaluated before they are interpreted.

From a practical perspective, classifiers scale very well over a large number of samples, while similarity measures can be troublesome in large datasets. For instance, training a classifier with five groups each with 100 samples is not much different than training a classifier with 20 groups each with 1,000 samples. And yet the number of pairwise comparisons to make in a similarity-based approach grows very quickly. The second case involves many, many more comparisons than the first. A common solution is to sample a fixed number of comparisons per group, for efficiency. Thus, we might calculate a thousand pairwise similarities between each dialect; this improves but does not remove the tractability problem.

The output of a similarity-based approach is thus a distribution of pairwise similarity measures between groups. We could simply take the mean of this distribution, but that would erase potentially important information. A realistic similarity-based approach, then, requires thinking about dialectal variation as a second-order set of distributions: the difference between American English and British English is a not a single measure (like 0.59) but rather a distribution of such measures, a sample from the underlying population. Here we use a sample of 1,000 pairwise comparisons and then calculate the Bayesian mean with a confidence interval of 95% to get the minimum and maximum similarity for each comparison.

If we work with similarities, we end up with a distance matrix in which each group has a similarity/distance to every other group within a given portion of the grammar. This can be viewed also as a graph so that graph-based measures can be calculated upon it. For instance, if we had 20 dialect groups this would give a distance matrix with 190 cells (ignoring self-similarity and assuming that syntactic similarity is symmetrical). This then needs to be converted into a graph where each dialect is a node and each part of the grammar is a type of edge and that edge weight is the estimated similarity (itself a distribution and not a single measure).

To summarize, we rely on two types of models to study syntactic variation: classifiers (supervised) and similarity measures (unsupervised). We evaluate the quality of both types of models using a prediction task, thus providing accuracy by class (like dialect) and by feature (like highly abstract constructions). Classifiers provide feature weights that tell us what parts of the grammar are in variation. They also provide error analysis to tell us what groups are easily confused (a confusion matrix). We primarily use classifiers to measure the magnitude of variation at each level of community structure in each portion of the grammar: for instance, where is syntactic variation located in the grammar? Similarity measures provide an estimated distance matrix which compares each group (like dialect) with every other group and with itself. This distance matrix is quite large at the scale of our experiments, so we further view this is a graph structure with nodes and edge weights. We primarily use similarity measures to take a more nuanced view of variation and to understand how diffusion operates across the network structure of the grammar itself.

1.6 Corpora: Observing Unelicited Production

For the experiments in this Element we use unelicited written corpora as evidence of the linguistic production of both individuals and groups of individuals. By *unelicited* we mean that these are naturally occurring texts that were created without any interventions by researchers (unlike dialect surveys or interviews, for instance). By *production* we mean that these corpora provide a sample of language use but no sample of dialect perception.

This section describes the two types of corpora used in these experiments: First, *geo-referenced corpora* which provide samples of the production of unique local populations; for this we use social media data (tweets). Second, *register-specific corpora* which are used to sample production within specific contexts; for this we use corpora representing a range of formal and informal contexts, from novels to newspaper comments. These corpora are listed by type in Table 1, with a brief description along with the number of words in each. A more detailed discussion of the methods involved in creating geo-referenced corpora follows in Section 1.7.

All corpora are divided into sentence-level units,[3] with tweets assumed to each contain a single sentence. In cases where the language of a sample is in question (i.e., with tweet collection), only samples identified as English by two state-of-the-art language identification models are retained (Dunn, 2020; Dunn & Nijhof, 2022). The same pre-processing is used for all corpora: removing non-alpha-numeric characters, case folding, separation of characters joined by punctuation (i.e., *country's* becomes *country s*), and removal of common templates like URLs and currencies.[4] This produces corpora which are comparable, with low-level orthographic differences like punctuation or capitalization which vary by register having been removed.

The advantage of a computational approach is scale: we can work with many populations across many contexts of usage. The disadvantage is meta-data: we know less about the demographics and the identity and the attitudes and the general cognitive abilities of each individual participant. For instance, we might have two speakers from the same local dialect, one who identifies closely with that local area and one who identifies as a global citizen without the same local attachments. We work with corpora from two conditions: first, *aggregated* corpora in which each sample represents an arbitrary selection of language users from the same place and, second, *individual* corpora in which each sample represents the production a single language user. We can use the individual-specific corpora, for example with measures of homogeneity, to determine how much internal variation there is within each local population.

Regardless, our analysis is not able to take into account what parts of the local population first adopt variants or refuse to alter their production to match the larger community. These kinds of questions require meta-data that is not available. But we can aks questions about (i) whether diffusion occurs equally across all nodes in the grammar; (ii) whether variation is stronger in the center or the periphery of the grammar; (iii) whether register variation is located in

3 https://github.com/explosion/spaCy.

4 https://github.com/jfilter/clean-text.

Table 1 List of corpora used in this element

Population-Specific Corpora		***Words***
Tweets, Individuals[a]	User-specific posts, UK and US	318 mil
Tweets, Populations[b]	Population-specific posts, UK and US	1.0 bil
Tweets, Global[b]	Population-specific posts, all countries	4.3 bil
Corpora from Register-Specific Sources		***Words***
Project Gutenberg[c]	Books published from 1850 to 1919	529 mil
EU Bookshop[d]	Contemporary nonfiction books	116 mil
Wikipedia[e]	Nonfiction articles	138 mil
Scientific Articles[f]	Published scientific articles	82 mil
European Parliament[d]	Speeches and legislative proceedings	56 mil
US Congress[g]	Speeches and legislative proceedings	84 mil
Print news[h]	Articles from the NYT (lead paragraphs)	92 mil
Online news	Articles from Politico and Business Insider	74 mil
Product Reviews[i]	Online product reviews	170 mil
Hotel Review[j]	Online hotel reviews	308 mil
News Comments[k]	Comments on newspaper articles	139 mil
Blogs[l]	Web-crawled blog posts	111 mil
Open Subtitles[m]	Dialogue from movies and television	198 mil
TED Talks[n]	Transcripts of public lectures	6.7 mil
Tweets[b]	Tweets from six countries	660 mil

[a] Grieve et al. (2019)

[b] Dunn (2020)

[c] Rae, Potapenko, Jayakumar, and Lillicrap (2020)

[d] Tiedemann (2012)

[e] Ortman (2018)

[f] Soares, Moreira, and Becker (2018)

[g] Gentzkow, Shapiro, and Taddy (2018)

[h] Parsons (2019)

[i] Zhang, Zhao, and LeCun (2015)

[j] Li (2012); McKenzie and Adams (2018)

[k] Kesarwani (2018)

[l] Schler, Koppel, Argamon, and Pennebaker (2006)

[m] Lison and Tiedemann (2016)

[n] Reimers and Gurevych (2020)

the same regions of the grammar as dialectal variation; and (iv) whether outer-circle communities vary in the same ways that more well-studied inner-circle communities vary. These are important questions which are not possible to ask without sufficient a scale of observation. And yet the trade-off of such scale is that we have less knowledge about perception and about language attitudes.

1.7 Networks: Structure within the Population

If variation is driven by our unique linguistic experiences, then differences in exposure will lead to differences in production. We have previously discussed the grammars and the data to be used; here we consider in more detail how to view the speech community as a network given geographic corpora. Geo-referenced social media posts (tweets) are used to represent the production of both (i) individuals and (ii) the background populations from which those individuals are drawn. Thus, we have corpora whose samples are aggregated tweets from just one person and corpora from the same places whose samples are tweets aggregated across many individuals. When we work with individuals vs dialect groups, we focus only on two inner-circle varieties (US and UK English). When we work with dialect groups alone, we focus on global data that includes many outer-circle populations from a total of fourteen countries.

The geographic social media corpora are constrained to the local areas around airports, as a proxy for urban areas: within 50km for the UK and within 50km or adjacent counties for the US. These approaches to spatial selection are governed by the meta-data available from the two existing corpora used: one collected between 2014 and 2017 (Grieve et al., 2019) and one between 2018 and 2022 (Dunn, 2020). The spatial areas represented in the two data sets overlap but the time period does not, so that there are no duplicate observations and no duplicate threads between the two corpora. This means that no portion of the individual-specific corpora is duplicated in the aggregated corpora.

The first corpus (2014–2017) is used to represent individuals: any single user who produces at least 50k words is included. Tweets are aggregated into samples of at least 2,500 words; thus, each individual is represented by at least 20 samples. This corpus contains samples from 6,744 individuals across the US and UK. The second corpus (2018–2022) is used to represent the local populations to which those individuals belong. This corpus represents the same locations in the US and the UK (c.f., Table 2), but at a different time period so that no samples overlap. While the adjacent time periods ensure there is no overlap in specific communicative situations (e.g., threads of tweets), the distance in time is short enough that we would not anticipate any grammatical

Table 2 Corpus size by country and region. *Population* refers to the size of the corpora which represent the background population for that location and *Individuals* of the corpora which represent individual users from that location. Only users with at least 20 samples of 2,500 words each are included.

			Population	**Individuals**
Region	**Example City**	**N. Cities**	***N. Words***	***N. Words***
US-1	Chicago	16	112.2 million	12.8 million
US-2	San Francisco	6	28.0 million	4.4 million
US-3	Dallas	8	72.3 million	11.1 million
US-4	Atlanta	7	63.0 million	5.3 million
US-5	Miami	5	37.2 million	3.8 million
US-6	Phoenix	5	53.1 million	5.7 million
US-7	New York	7	94.8 million	7.9 million
US-8	Kansas City	7	53.9 million	2.0 million
US-9	Los Angeles	5	41.1 million	10.4 million
Total:	*United States*	*66*	*556.0 million*	*63.7 million*
UK-1	London	7	161.5 million	18.3 million
UK-2	Birmingham	9	145.6 million	8.8 million
UK-3	Edinburgh	4	21.3 million	3.7 million
UK-4	Manchester	5	157.5 million	9.6 million
UK-5	Belfast	2	13.9 million	1.0 million
Total:	*United Kingdom*	*27*	*500.0 million*	*41.7 million*

change to have occurred between the two periods. This second corpus is also divided into samples of 2,500 words, with tweets from the same place being combined into samples.

These two data sets are thus comparable in every way except that one is aggregated by individual and one by time and place. We take this to represent both (i) variation across individuals from the same population and (ii) variation within the larger populations from which those individuals are drawn. The overview of the corpora is shown in Table 2: the US is divided into nine regional dialects and the UK into five. Each region is composed of multiple metro areas; note that all data here is collected from urban areas to avoid rural-urban divides in density. The corpora representing populations are the largest (at 554 million words for the US and 471 million for the UK), though the corpora representing individuals remain large as well (at 182 million words for the US and 135 million words for the UK).

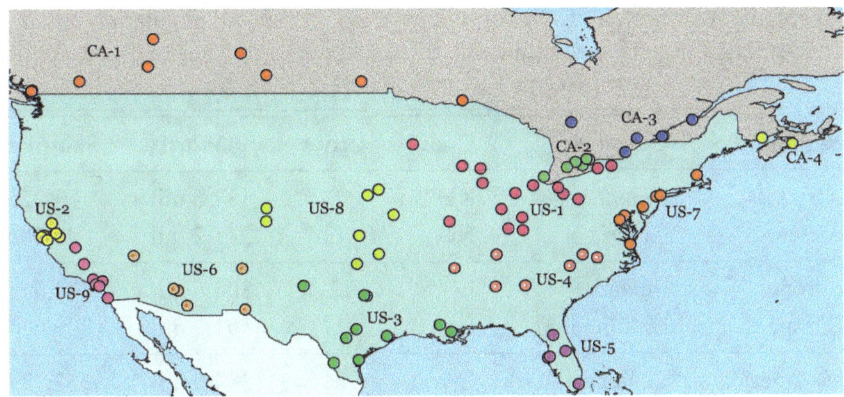

Figure 2 Map of local populations represented in the US and Canada.

Local populations are represented by the nearest airport; because of ease of movement within urban areas, this city-level grouping is the most fine-grained spatial distinction available from corpora. This spatial hierarchy has three tiers: (1) the country (US vs UK), (2) the region (Midwest vs West Coast), and (3) the specific metro area (e.g., Indianapolis vs Chicago). The first and third levels are pre-defined because they derive from nation-states and city locations. For the second, we use the density-based H-DBSCAN algorithm to clusters metro areas into regional groups (Campello, Moulavi, & Sander, 2013; Campello et al., 2015). A refinement of the DBSCAN, this algorithm groups points spatially into local clusters, where each point is an airport. The result is a set of regional areas within a country. For example, the nine areas within the United States are shown in Figure 2, where each color represents a different group. Manual adjustments of unclustered or borderline points is then undertaken to produce the final clusters; these are visualized and available as spatial files in the supplementary materials.

This three-level hierarchy of populations is shown in Table 2, with US regions on the top and UK regions on the bottom. An example city is given for each region id, drawn from the most frequent city within each region. Thus, the region US-1 refers to the Midwest, with the exemplar city being Chicago. The number of metro areas within each region is also shown; for example, US-1 contains sixteen metro areas, each defined geographically by its airport.

The corpora used for global variation in English is an expansion of the population-based corpora described above, but including more countries around the world. It thus follows the same three-tiered spatial organization: by country, by region, and by local metro area. Regions are again based on spatial clustering. This leads to corpora representing 14 different countries, with a

Table 3 Distribution of sub-corpora by region for global population-based dataset. Each sample is a unique sub-corpus which aggregates tweets from the same place into a document of 2,500 words.

Region	Country	Code	Cities	Words	Samples
Africa	Kenya	KE	6	183.6 mil	73,225
Africa	Nigeria	NG	13	241.2 mil	96,186
Europe	Ireland	IE	2	308.6 mil	123,071
Europe	U. Kingdom	UK	27	501.7 mil	200,025
N. America	Canada	CA	23	384.0 mil	153,124
N. America	U. States	US	72	557.8 mil	222,422
Oceania	Australia	AU	15	512.8 mil	204,369
Oceania	New Zealand	NZ	6	186.1 mil	74,227
S. Asia	Bangladesh	BD	5	119.5 mil	47,667
S. Asia	India	IN	56	384.4 mil	153,311
S. Asia	Pakistan	PK	15	273.8 mil	109,209
SE. Asia	Indonesia	ID	29	115.8 mil	46,187
SE. Asia	Malaysia	MY	17	173.5 mil	69,209
SE. Asia	Philippines	PH	18	213.8 mil	85,271
	Totals	**14**	**304**	**4.15 bil**	**1.65 mil**

total of 304 local metro areas grouped into 54 regions, as shown in Table 3. The corpus as a whole has 4.16 billion words or 1.66 million samples. Some countries are better represented than others, however: the US, UK, and India all have over 250k samples while Cameroon has only 4.9k and Uganda 3.3k. For this reason we are careful to measure confidence bounds for each estimated similarity value, so that areas with fewer samples are not represented by a simple mean if there is high variance present.

To summarize this section, we have three variants of tweet-based corpora which operationalize the population network in different ways: (i) individual-specific samples from the US and the UK divided into local areas; (ii) population-level samples from the US and the UK divided into the same local areas and not overlapping in time; (iii) population-level samples created in the same manner as the second corpus but containing samples from fourteen countries in order to provide a more realistic global model of variation in English.

2 Variation across Individuals

We turn now to our first case-study: individual variation within local populations in the US and UK. We start by presenting a usage-based view in which the unique linguistic experience of individuals leads to unique grammars. The case-study itself focuses on identifying individual differences and measuring where such differences are located in the grammar. We end by comparing individual-specific corpora with aggregated corpora from the same local dialects. Much work in computational sociolinguistics depends on aggregated corpora and this experiment allows us to validate the degree to which aggregated and individual-specific samples agree on the uniqueness of local dialects.

We start by using classification-based experiments to measure the magnitude of individual variation and determine where in the grammar it is located. To do this, we train separate classifiers for each city to identify individuals from that city. Thus, we are relying on different nodes within the grammar to distinguish between individuals from the same local dialects producing language in the same register. We then use similarity-based experiments to model the structure of variation without training samples. We use the homogeneity of individuals from the same population as a measure of the amount of individual differences. We then undertake a regression analysis to determine whether factors like population contact and language contact are able to explain why some local dialects are more homogeneous than others, where homogeneity means that speakers from a given population are more similar.

2.1 Individual Experiences Lead to Individual Differences

From a usage-based perspective, an individual's grammar emerges given exposure to usage. In this context, *usage* is simply the production of other speakers. Two individuals from the same city are likely to have highly overlapping exposure: they experience the same local dialect, the same language contact situations, the same media sources, and so on. As a result, individual differences in the grammar should be weaker than population-based differences because the differences in exposure during learning are smaller within the same local population. Our operationalization of exposure is the observed production of others within the same register (social media).

We have divided the grammar into different types of constructions based on (i) the level of abstraction, (ii) the order of emergence, and (iii) the degree of centrality. Constructions are expected to be learned first as more concrete and item-specific representations which are then generalized into higher order constructions. Thus, we hypothesize that two speakers from the same local dialect should differ in the specific low-level constructions they are exposed to but should reach similar higher-order generalizations. In the same way, we hypothesize that constructions on the periphery are subject to individual differences, while constructions in the core of the grammar are more stable.

The presence of individual differences in the grammar has been to some degree ignored within linguistics, with its focus on forming generalizations about a language which require consistency within a speech community. The presence of individual differences, however, has been robustly established within the field of forensic linguistics which is focused precisely on leveraging individual differences for practical purposes (Nini, 2023). Further, although much work seeks to generalize over individual differences, it remains the case that even experimental work must grapple with their presence (Kidd & Donnelly, 2020). From a usage-based perspective, however, such differences are expected because speakers have different levels of entrenchment for even those constructions which they share (Langacker, 1987). Beyond entrenchment, minor differences in slot-constraints can lead to constructions with slightly different patterns of production. Since each construction has many slot-constraints, this leads to a large number of minor individual differences in the grammar. If this usage-based view is correct, we should see high accuracy in lower-order constructions (learned directly from exposure) but lower accuracy in higher-order constructions (generalized on top of lower-order constructions).

2.2 Magnitude and Robustness: How Much Individual Variation?

We use a classifier to measure the magnitude and robustness of individual variation by comparing the production of different users within the same city. This kind of model learns to connect variants with individuals; the goal is to distinguish between samples that represent different users. Thus, a higher prediction accuracy indicates that there is more variation because individuals are more easily identified. In general, classes that are difficult to distinguish are more similar and those which are easy to tell apart are more different. We further use cross-validation to ensure that accuracy is consistent across different sets of samples, to avoid overfitting any one part of the corpus. More consistent accuracy across folds indicates that the variation is robust because it does not depend on a specific set of samples.

For this and future classification-based experiments, we use a Linear Support Vector Machine (SVM). The experimental design discussed in this section remains consistent across individual differences (users within the same city), local and national dialects (aggregated samples from different regions and

Table 4 Break-down of classification tasks. The number of classes refers to the labels present in each instance of the classifier. Thus, for individual differences, the classifier only observes fourteen users at a time even if more users are available.

Level	Classes	Prediction Task
Individuals	14	Users within the same city (e.g., users in Birmingham UK)
Dialects-Local	6	Local dialects in the same region (e.g., Chicago vs Milwaukee in North America)
Dialects-National	14	Country-level dialects defined by nation states (e.g., US vs UK, both Inner-Circle)
Registers	15	Distinct registers within the same modality (e.g., Wikipedia vs Reviews, written and digital)

countries), and context (samples from different written registers). This consistency makes it possible to compare the magnitude and location of each type of syntactic variation. A break-down of the range of classification tasks is given in Table 4, ranging from individual differences at the top to registers at the bottom. With the exception of local dialect classification, all levels of variation are constrained to the same number of classes to make the results directly comparable.[5]

To support this comparison, we fix the number of individuals per city at fourteen, so that the number of classes can be the same across cities with different numbers of samples. For instance, Chicago is represented by almost 20x the number of individuals as Minneapolis; by constraining the numbers of users observe, we make these cities directly comparable. The task is to distinguish between fourteen arbitrary individuals from the same city. This task is then repeated ten times with different sets of individuals, as described below, to provide a better estimate of individual differences within each local dialect community.

The question is not just the magnitude and robustness of syntactic variation in written registers but also where in the grammar that variation is located. Thus, we train nine separate classifiers, one for each nodes within the grammar

[5] Local dialects involve classifying cities within the same region, like Chicago vs Milwaukee in the Midwest. However, some outer-circle dialects have only a few cities per region; we decided to focus on making inner-circle and outer-circle regions comparable rather than making local dialects fit with the other tasks.

as shown in Figure 1. The prediction accuracy of each part of the grammar, measured using the f-score, allows us to observe the magnitude and robustness of individual variation across different portions of the grammar. The higher the prediction accuracy, the more variation there is in that portion of the grammar. Thus, if lower-levels of abstraction have a higher f-score, this means that individuals are more different in these more concrete constructions but more similar in abstract families of constructions.

Because we are working with large corpora, we are able to estimate classification accuracy across many samples. First, for each of the classification problems in Table 4 we take ten rounds that each work with a different sub-set of the data. For individual differences, this means that for each round we take a random sample of fourteen individuals from a given city. Thus, these results do not rely on a single small set of users. This replication of the experiment across ten rounds of arbitrary users allows us to calculate a confidence interval for the results. Within each round, we use five-fold cross-validation to estimate the classifier performance. This again provides a sample of classification accuracy across different permutations of the data within each round; cross-validation ensures that all samples rotate between the testing set and the training set so that the classifier does not over-fit a specific testing set.

We thus are estimating classification accuracy across fifty individual classifiers for each city (ten by selection of users and five by cross-validation within each set of users). The reported values are a Bayesian estimate of the mean f-score with a confidence interval of 95%. For example, in Table 5, the f-score of individual classification using the first-order portion of the grammar has a minimum value of 0.98 and a maximum value of 0.99. This provides both magnitude (number of errors) and robustness (variation in magnitude). In other words, magnitude is the estimated prediction accuracy and robustness is the variation in prediction accuracy. The results in this table are aggregated by country; the full city-level results are available in the supplementary material.

With reference to the results in Table 5, it is clear that there is a tremendous amount of individual syntactic variation in written data representing these local dialects: even when drawing individuals from the same location the model is easily able to distinguish between them. In fact, one motivation for including similarity measures in this Element is that the sheer amount of variation leads to a ceiling effect for these classifiers: performance reaches the maximum possible accuracy in several conditions. Thus, these results show that the magnitude of individual variation within cities is high. Further, the robustness is also relatively high: we might expect, for instance, that some cities or some individuals would be distinct and thus easily identified, but that other cities or individuals would have lower accuracy. Here we see, however, that the minimum

Table 5 Classification accuracy for individual differences as represented by the f-score for distinguishing users within the same city. The min and max values are estimated using a Bayesian confidence interval of 95% across five-fold cross-validation across ten unique sets of users. Each classifier observes fourteen users with a comparable number of samples; these users are chosen at random for each of ten rounds. Countries are represented by the mean across cities; full results by city are available in the supplementary material. All values are significantly higher than the majority baseline.

Level of Abstraction						
	First-Order		**Third-Order**		**Fourth-Order**	
	Min	***Max***	***Min***	***Max***	***Min***	***Max***
US	0.98	0.99	0.87	0.90	0.70	0.73
UK	0.97	0.98	0.88	0.90	0.78	0.79
Order of Emergence						
	LEX		SYN		SEM+	
	Min	***Max***	***Min***	***Max***	***Min***	***Max***
US	0.97	0.98	0.96	0.97	0.97	0.98
UK	0.96	0.97	0.95	0.96	0.94	0.96
Degree of Centrality						
	Low		**Mid**		**High**	
	Min	***Max***	***Min***	***Max***	***Min***	***Max***
US	0.98	0.99	0.97	0.98	0.87	0.90
UK	0.98	0.98	0.95	0.96	0.90	0.92

and maximum estimates (with a 95% confidence interval) are generally within one point. This means that our estimates of individual uniqueness are quite robust.

At the same time, we are aggregating across many cities in many regions of the US and the UK, and there are some exceptions to this level of accuracy. For instance, in London the cross-fold f-score for the high-frequency core constructions ranges from 0.89 to 0.94, a fairly wide range. In Newcastle, however, this range is only between 0.95 and 0.97. So, London has fewer individual differences in this part of the grammar than Newcastle. For our purposes, we are viewing individual differences within each city as a sample of the underlying population within each country; thus, the results in Table 5 are aggregated to show that country-level estimate. The point is that there is a great deal of syntactic variation even across individuals and even in written registers. A deeper exploration of city-level variation in the amount of individual differences follows in the next sections.

These country-specific estimates of the magnitude of individual variation show that individual differences are much stronger in specific parts of the grammar. Starting with level of abstraction, there is a consistent trend that more concrete (lower level) constructions differ more between individuals. First-order constructions (the most concrete) obtain a minimum f-score of 0.98 in the US and 0.97 in the UK. This high level of accuracy indicates that individuals are generally quite easy to tell apart given syntactic production. At the next level of abstraction, this minimum f-score falls to 0.87 (US) and 0.88 (UK), a significant drop. And, finally, within the most abstract constructions, the minimum f-score drops further to 0.70 (US) and 0.78 (UK). This means that individual differences across both dialects are concentrated in the most item-specific and surface-level constructions. Interestingly, the two dialects score quite closely until we reach fourth-order constructions, in which case the UK has a much higher score. This indicates that the US has fewer high-level differences than the UK.

For order of emergence, on the other hand, there is no significant difference between early-stage and late-stage constructions: the confidence intervals overlap. This means that a representation-based division of the grammar has no impact at all on the model, which in turn means that individual differences are not organized by order of emergence. Within degree of centrality, there is no difference between constructions on the periphery and those in the main part of the grammar. However, performance falls significantly for high-frequency core constructions (although not to the same level as highly abstract constructions). This means that within the core grammar there is less variation across individuals than in the rest of the grammar; this effect is smaller than for level of abstraction in terms of magnitude and robustness.

This section has used classification experiments to determine how much variation there is across individual users and how consistent or robust that level of variation is. Our first conclusion is that there is a tremendous amount of syntactic variation in these written registers. At the same time, this variation is not distributed evenly across the grammar: level of abstraction has a strong and significant impact, with most variation contained in more concrete and lower-level constructions. This effect is not seen at all for order of emergence and only slightly for degree of centrality. While all cases remain significantly higher than the baseline, this indicates that individual variation is concentrated in specific parts of the grammar network.

2.3 Evaluating Individual Similarity Measures

The results in the previous section relied on a classifier; in this section we detail the methodology for measuring similarity between conditions (i.e., between individuals within the same city). The distinction between these two approaches to variation, at a conceptual level, was presented in Section 1.5. Here we focus on the specific details of the similarity measures and then compare a classification-based and a similarity-based model of variation. Our focus here is on validating the similarity measures using a classification task: are individuals from one city more similar to one another than to individuals from other near-by cities? Thus, this validation task measures how much confidence we should have in these unsupervised measures; it looks much like a classification task, in that we are predicting categories (same vs different). However, the purpose is to ensure that the measure is valid before we dig deeper into individual differences in the next section. The combination of classifiers (supervised) and similarity measures (unsupervised) here provides converging evidence that further strengthens our understanding of syntactic variation.

For working with a large set of features, as we are here, a similarity value can become overwhelmed by small differences in very frequent features. Thus, we adopt a pipeline which controls for the absolute frequency of constructions, as shown in Figure 3. First, we start with the token frequencies (usage) of constructions in each sample. These are the basic observable. Second, we standardize frequencies across the entire corpus so that our representation of each sample controls for the expected frequency of each construction. Thus, a very common construction will not have more impact than an uncommon construction because we are focusing on differences from the expected (z-score standardized) frequency. A high value means that a construction is used more in this sample than in most samples and a low value means that a construction

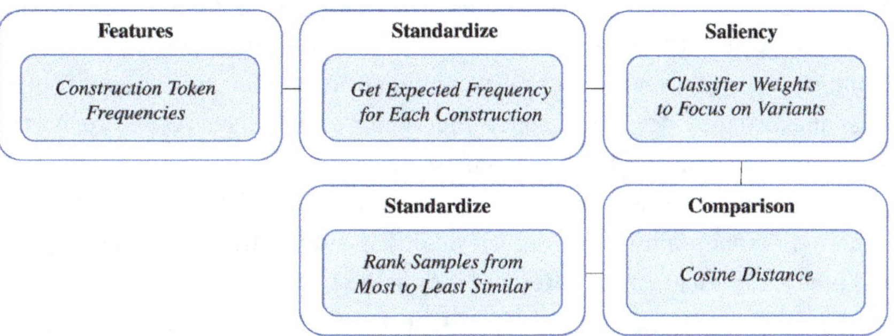

Figure 3 Pipeline for measuring similarity between conditions, whether based on samples from dialects or registers.

is used less often than expected. Third, we take the classifier weights from the Linear SVM used to measure the magnitude of variation to focus the similarity measure on more salient constructions. We take the mean absolute feature weight as an indication of the degree to which each construction is subject to variation; a high weight means that the construction has positive predictive power and a low weight means that the construction has negative predictive power. By taking the absolute value across all classes, we are taking information about the degree to which a construction varies but not about the way in which it varies. This enables the similarity measure to focus on the most salient constructions for modeling variation. Fourth, cosine distance is used to represent the similarity of samples, with high values indicating large differences and small values indicating small differences. Fifth, to make the comparison robust across both locations and nodes within the grammar, we standardize the cosine distances. This provides a rank of all samples from the most similar to the least similar that accounts for the average distance between samples. Thus, a distance of 2.0 would be two standard deviations above the mean distance. This final standardization is helpful for interpreting and comparing distance measures across specific experiments. The end result of this pipeline is a rank, for each experiment, of the most similar samples to the least similar samples.

We are interested in estimating the difference between individuals rather than between individual samples. Instead of calculating a single similarity measure between conditions, then, we draw samples from the population of pairwise comparisons to ensure robustness. This means that rather than calculating a single difference between individuals in London and individuals in Manchester, we sample a population of comparisons, each based on a unique pair of subcorpora. For dialects (local and national) and for registers, we sample 1,000 pairwise similarity measures in order to estimate the similarity between conditions (i.e., between social media and news articles). For individuals, we sample a population of fifty pairs; this smaller number is chosen because there are many individuals and less data per individual. The pipeline shown in Figure 3 is thus repeated fifty times per condition, each time comparing two different samples of usage. Much like cross-validation in a classifier, this ensures robustness and also provides a confidence interval for our estimate. As before, we use a Bayesian estimate with a 95% confidence interval.

To calculate accuracy for individuals, we calculate the similarity between each individual within a city and (i) other individuals from the same city and (ii) other individuals from different cities in the same region. For instance, this would compare the similarity within Chicago with Chicago vs Indianapolis. We then take the minimum and maximum similarity estimates. When there is no overlap between same-city and different-city comparisons, the measure

Table 6 Accuracy of unsupervised similarity measures for categorizing individuals within vs between local dialects. Measure in accuracy (percent correct). A correct categorization makes individuals from a local dialect (like Chicago) more similar to one another than to individuals from other dialects from the same region. Results are aggregated across all cities in a region.

	Emergence			**Abstraction**			**Centrality**		
	LEX	SYN	FULL	*1st*	*3rd*	*4th*	LOW	MID	HIGH
UK-1	97.6	97.6	88.1	97.6	88.1	73.8	97.6	73.8	78.6
UK-2	98.6	95.8	98.6	100	81.9	86.1	100	70.8	80.6
UK-3	100	100	91.7	100	100	83.3	100	75.0	75.0
UK-4	75.0	95.0	80.0	100	70.0	55.0	100	95.0	75.0
UK-5	100	100	100	100	100	100	100	100	100
US-1	91.3	86.7	89.2	94.6	91.7	81.3	91.3	95.8	82.5
US-2	90.0	76.7	80.0	93.3	83.3	96.7	96.7	90.0	80.0
US-3	86.1	90.3	87.5	87.5	84.7	88.9	83.3	84.7	84.7
US-4	97.6	95.2	95.2	100	92.9	71.4	95.2	83.3	73.8
US-5	100	100	100	100	100	75.0	100	95.0	95.0
US-6	95.0	85.0	100	100	85.0	85.0	100	100	90.0
US-7	88.1	83.3	85.7	92.9	81.0	76.2	92.9	90.5	90.5
US-8	100	100	100	100	95.2	92.9	100	100	92.9
US-9	75.0	60.0	80.0	85.0	75.0	55.0	80.0	90.0	50.0
AVG	*92.4*	*90.4*	*91.1*	*96.4*	*87.7*	*80.0*	*95.5*	*88.8*	*82.0*

makes a correct prediction. In other words, it correctly identifies that there is a significant difference between individuals in the same city and individuals not in the same city. This validation measure is focused only partly on individual differences; it does, however, provide an accuracy-based measure of how good the similarity measures are.

The results in Table 6 show the mean accuracy per region for the US and UK. Accuracy varies by both the part of the grammar used to measure similarity and the region in question. For instance, UK-5 (i.e., Belfast) has a much higher accuracy than UK-4 (i.e., Manchester). This means that even using an unsupervised model the one region is more coherent or homogeneous than the other. The model is unsupervised because the similarity measure has no training data and thus no meta-linguistic knowledge. The measure reported is accuracy.

Notice, first, that the level of accuracy is generally quite high. For instance, the accuracy of early-stage lexical constructions is 92.4% and for more concrete first-order constructions is 96.4% and for low-frequency peripheral constructions is 95.5%. This shows that there is, again, tremendous syntactic variation across individuals in this data even with an unsupervised model. With more geographic precision, we also see variation here across areas. For instance, in the US regions 5 (Miami) and 6 (Phoenix) have a high accuracy across parts of the grammar while regions 7 (New York) and 9 (Los Angeles) have lower accuracy. Lower accuracy means that it is more difficult to determine whether two individuals are from the same city. This could indicate, for instance, that both New York and Los Angeles are more heterogeneous, thus making it difficult to separate them from other local dialects in the area. This will be explored further in the next sections.

Our other question is whether some parts of the grammar are subject to more variation at the individual level. As before, level of abstraction has a clear pattern where more concrete constructions have the most variation (96.4% accuracy), while the most abstract constructions have the least (80.0% accuracy). Also as before, order of emergence does not have a significant difference, so that individual differences are not more or less concentrated in one part of the grammar; in fact, the accuracy is relatively high in all three categories.

For degree of centrality, the classification results showed no clear distinction within the two noncore categories (mid-frequency and low-frequency), but do show a strong difference between noncore and core constructions. That same distinction is replicated here, with core constructions having less variation as indicated by a lower prediction accuracy. The difference is that, with similarity measures, the mid category is distinguished from peripheral constructions. Why? For the classifier, performance is so high that there is no space left for peripheral and noncore constructions to behave differently. With similarity measures, however, the observed range of accuracy is larger. We can conclude that evidence from supervised and unsupervised models converges onto the observation that individual syntactic variation is stronger in more concrete and more peripheral constructions and weaker in more abstract and core constructions. This convergence is important because it means that the underlying conclusion can be replicated across different families of models and across many different cities.

This section has described the similarity measures used to compare conditions and validated them on a classification task. Because these are unsupervised models, it is absolutely essential that we validate the similarity measures. Given that these measures have been shown to be highly accurate, we will proceed to use them to observe differences between individuals in order to further understand how such individual differences are organized in the grammar.

Perhaps more importantly, the predictions which usage-based theories make about individual differences are shown to be correct: this type of variation is concentrated in less abstract and more peripheral constructions. From the perspective of the emergence of grammar, individuals learn first-order constructions directly from exposure, and individuals all have slightly different linguistic experiences. Higher-order constructions, however, are formed partly based on exposure and partly by generalizing on top of entrenched first-order constructions. Thus, individuals have different grammars in more surface-level constructions (on the lexical side of the continuum) but reach similar generalizations in more schematic constructions (on the syntactic side of the continuum).

2.4 Exploring Individual Differences

We have seen that there are significant individual differences in written registers across many cities. We have also seen that similarity measures can be accurate for distinguishing individuals from the same and from different cities. Here we focus on the amount of internal variation within a city. The usage-based view of language expects that different linguistic experiences will lead to minor differences in item-specific and peripheral constructions, and this view was supported by the previous results. We can go further: not only do we expect that there are individual differences within each local dialect, we also expect that cities will have different rates of individual differences if those differences are in fact caused by different exposure situations. For instance, cities with more language contact situations should have differing amounts of homogeneity because there will be more variation in the linguistic experience of specific individuals.

We calculate homogeneity by first taking all similarity values between individuals to construct a standardized space using the z-score. This tells us what range of similarity measures we should observe. Second, we compare individuals within the same city within this standardized space. A low value (negative) means that individuals are more similar than the average and a high value (positive) means that individuals are more different than the average. The reason that positive means different and negative means similar is that the measure is based on cosine distance.

This is shown for the US in Figure 4 with a randomly selected city to represent each region. These are violin plots showing the distribution of pairs of individuals; previous aggregated measures reported the mean (here shown by a white bar). These plots instead show the range of pairs. We notice, first, that some cities have an almost bimodal distribution; for instance both Fresno and

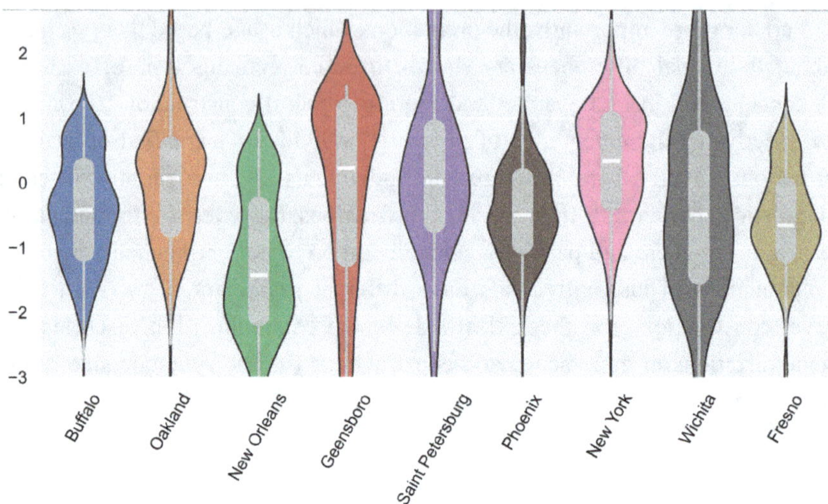

Figure 4 Homogeneity of individuals within cities for the US with late-stage SEM+ constructions.

New Orleans have a large cluster around the mean and then another smaller cluster higher up. This reflects communities within the community. Second, we notice that some cities (like Greensboro) are more hetergeneous, with a higher distance overall. This means that places differ in the magnitude of individual differences internally. And, third, we see that there is much more variance in some places (like Wichita) than others (like Phoenix). This suggests that these cities, also, are more heterogeneous. This figure shows the late-stage SEM+ constructions; the full range of figures by country and node of the grammar are available in the supplementary material.

This approach to individual differences accounts for location (dialect) and register, but it does not include social factors like age or ethnicity or gender or class. What does that mean for our analysis of individual differences, if the data does not account for factors known to influence syntactic production? First, the data here is drawn from tweets and this social media platform has a somewhat different demographic representation than we would expect given the population as a whole. This means that we are not sampling equally from all social groups within each place. On the other hand, it is reasonable to assume given previous work (Grieve et al., 2019) that this social skew is consistent across places. In other words, tweets may better represent middle-age males, but this skew is consistent so that we are observing the same comparable sub-set of the population across cities and regions.

We can therefore assume that the selection of individuals that are sampled from each city comes from the same population of social groups, with the same mix of genders and ages, for example. The distance measures are standardized to contextualize what a high and low similarity actually are, and this standardization takes into account social variation in the sense that individuals are drawn randomly from the population of Twitter users in each location. For one city to be more or less homogeneous, then, tells us something about variation in that city which goes beyond predictable social differences (which should be more or less consistent across each city in the US or the UK). For this reason, we can think about the analysis in this section as individual differences that control for register and place (explicitly) as well as social variation (implicitly).

Given the varying levels of individual differences by city shown in Figure 4, our next question is whether we can explain this variation. Why do some populations exhibit more syntactic differences between individuals? To answer this question, we use a linear mixed effects regression to determine which factors are explanatory. The dependent variable here is the mean self-similarity or homogeneity; this is the center of each violin plot in the figure. We use region (such as Midwest vs East Coast American English) as a random effect. This controls for different levels of homogeneity by place and allows us to focus on the contribution of specific factors more generally.

We use five independent variables: First, one question is whether exposure to other dialects and other languages is a source of variation. Thus, we take an estimate of total air travel between cities (Huang et al., 2013) as a proxy for the social connections between two places. We extract two independent variables from this: the percentage of incoming travel that is from the same country (mostly representing different dialects of the same language) and the percentage of incoming travel that is from the same region (representing a finer-scale of dialect contact). Second, we might expect that larger urban areas are simply more diverse which, in turn, causes more distinct linguistic experiences. We capture this using the raw number of incoming travelers as a proxy for population size: larger and more diverse cities will have more incoming travelers. Third, we might expect that language contact within a city also leads to individual differences. Since we are observing the Twitter-using population, we build a corpus of all tweets within 200km of each city and estimate the percentage of the corpus represented by different languages. This provides an indication of the market share of each language, or how much of the total digital discourse it represents. This is converted into a single scalar measure using the Herfindahl-Hirschmann Index or HHI (Dunn, Coupe, & Adams, 2020). A high HHI indicates a monopoly of one language (almost always English here) and a low HHI indicates a diverse set of languages. We use two variants of this measure: one with English and one without English. This distinction provides

Table 7 Significance values from a Linear Mixed Effects model with region as a random effect and explanatory variables (shown in the Table) as fixed effects. Cities with less exposure to international populations are less homogeneous.

	Level of Abstraction		
	First	***Third***	***Fourth***
Percent of Travel Within Country	**0.001** (-)	**0.003** (-)	ns
Percent of Travel Within Region	ns	ns	ns
Size (N. Travelers)	ns	ns	ns
Linguistic Diversity	ns	ns	ns
	Order of Emergence		
	LEX	SYN	SEM+
Percent of Travel Within Country	**0.000** (-)	**0.001** (-)	**0.000** (-)
Percent of Travel Within Region	0.056	ns	ns
Size (N. Travelers)	ns	ns	ns
Linguistic Diversity	0.048	ns	ns
	Degree of Centrality		
	Low	***Mid***	***High***
Percent of Travel Within Country	**0.000** (-)	ns	ns
Percent of Travel Within Region	ns	ns	ns
Size (N. Travelers)	ns	ns	ns
Linguistic Diversity	ns	ns	ns

a finer view of language contact within each city. These last two variables are shown as a single *Linguistic Diversity* row in the results.

The significance of these factors for explaining variations in homogeneity across cities is shown in Table 7. The four main factors are repeated within each division of the grammar. Significant p-values are provided and marked in bold. Only one factor is consistently significant: the percentage of travel that is within the same country. The coefficient here is negative, which in this case means that cities with less international travel have lower rates of individual differences. For example, Indianapolis is quite homogeneous and also has little international travel (the travel dataset accounts for multiple stop itineraries so it is not relevant whether a given city has an international airport). We are using the amount of incoming air travel from the same or different countries as a proxy for the aggregate amount of long-distance contact which a local population is subject to. This kind of contact and the exposure situations that it creates is significantly related to homogeneity: local populations with less international contact have fewer individual variations.

Note that neither operationalization of linguistic diversity are significant here. Why is there a distinction between the linguistic landscape of a place (what languages are used) and how much contact there is with international populations? In the first case, there is contact with other languages and in the second case there is contact with speakers of another language who are not necessarily using that language (L2 speakers of English, for instance). This latter factor is more important for explaining the grammatical homogeneity of a population. We visualize the goodness-of-fit of this model by plotting the residual errors in Figure 5. Each point is a local city whose syntactic self-similarity is being explained (US cities are marked with a circle and UK cities with an x). The red line indicates the ideal location for all points if the model were entirely accurate; thus, distance from the line represents unexplained variance in homogeneity. Positive values mean that a city is more heterogeneous than expected and negative values that a city is more homogeneous than expected.

First, we notice that US cities are generally better explained by this model. For instance, this could indicate a greater difference between individuals in the UK that is not captured by travel patterns. Further, it could also be the case

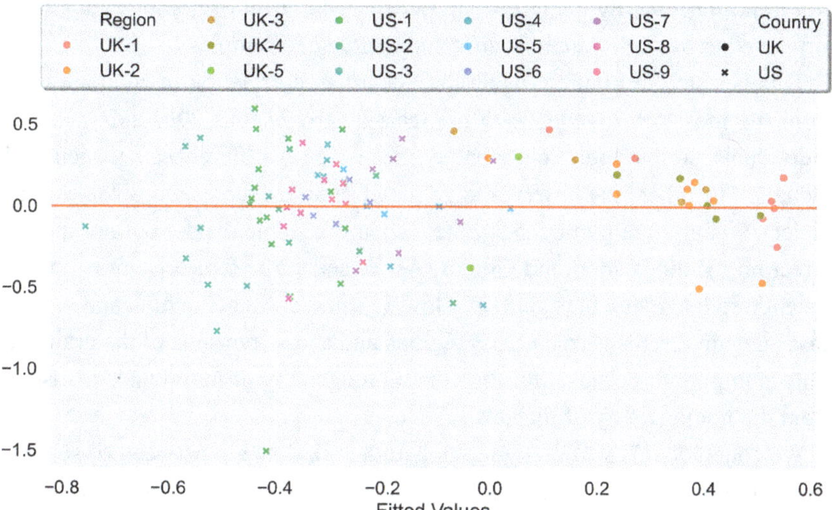

Figure 5 Plot of residual errors for regression explaining homogeneity of individuals within the same city. US cities are indicated with a circle and UK cities with an x. Points closer to the red line are more accuracy and points further away are less accurate.

that air travel is a better proxy for contact within the US than within the UK. Within the UK, the points furthest from the line usually belong to the UK-1 region, which is essentially the area surrounding London.

With these outlying points aside, the model can generally explain syntactic self-similarity across individuals using the amount of domestic vs international travel. More individual differences arise, then, when contact with nondomestic populations increases but not necessarily contact with non-English languages (c.f., the HHI variable is not a significant predictor). In other words, contact across more different varieties leads to individuals with less homogeneous experiences which then leads to individual differences in their grammars. This is a further piece of evidence about the importance of individual linguistic experiences in the emergence of the grammar.

To what degree do these results reflect the amount of individual differences in a local population as opposed to properties of that dialect itself? We have been working with two distinct sets of tweets: the first is collected by individuals in which each sample is produced by a single person and in which homogeneity (self-similarity) represents differences between individuals in the same city. The second set of tweets, on the other hand, is created by aggregated samples from the same time and place which do not represent a single individual. We would expect that the first corpus captures individual differences while the second corpus would average away individual differences, leaving us with a representation of geographic dialect. In this case, we would expect that there would not necessarily be agreement between the level of homogeneity at the city level across individual-specific and aggregated samples.

This is tested in Figure 6 using the Spearman correlation to compare cities from the most heterogeneous to the least heterogeneous. One side observes individuals, so that high homogeneity means fewer differences between individuals. The other side observes aggregated samples, representing the average dialect, so that high homogeneity means a more stable dialect but not making direct implications about individuals. As we see in the figure, there is no consistent trend: agreement is generally low, in some cases being high and in other cases negative. This is true across regions and across portions of the grammar. This is important because it means that homogeneity of individuals is distinct from the homogeneity of dialects.

We conclude this section by looking at the relationship between (i) samples from individual members of a dialect and (ii) aggregated samples of a dialect that represent many individuals. The first retains individual and social differences while the second will average away variation that is not dialectal. Given the high accuracy shown in previous sections for classifying local dialects, we extend this further by training the model under two conditions: first, training

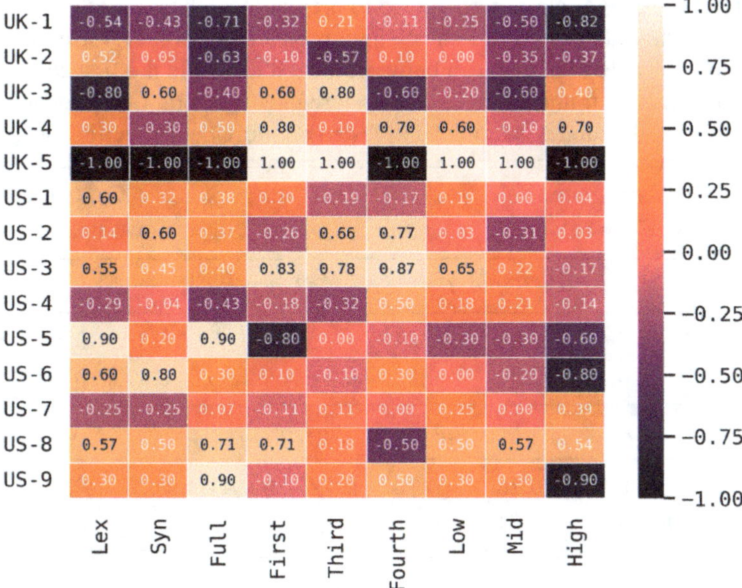

Figure 6 Agreement between homogeneity of individuals and homogeneity of aggregated samples by part of the grammar and region. This shows that the individual corpora are distinct from the population-based corpora, reflecting individual differences rather than dialect.

on aggregated samples from local dialects (which average away individual and social differences) and then testing the model on the same kind of corpora; second, training on samples from individuals and testing on samples from other individuals. Our question is the degree to which dialectal variation in these individuals remains visible to the model in spite of individual and social differences also being present; this is represented by the difference in accuracy between the two conditions.

To test this we train a classifier under a similar condition as in the investigation of the magnitude and location of individual differences: for each country we train a model to predict regional dialects within that country. For instance, this would mean predicting Midwest American English vs East Coast American English. We do this using a Linear SVM; the classifier is trained from one city in the region, chosen at random, and then tested on held-out samples from that same city. We repeat this pipeline ten times, each with a randomly chosen city to represent each region, so that the averaged results are robust over specific cities. To keep the classifier comparable across countries, we use only five regions per model (the maximum available in the UK).

The results in Table 8 show the difference in the predictability of local dialects within aggregated vs individual-specific corpora. The performance is

Table 8 F-Score of classifiers trained to predict local dialects given different types of input. High scores indicate high prediction accuracy, meaning that the model is able to distinguish between local dialects. In the first condition, the model is trained and tested on aggregated corpora. In the second condition, the model is trained and tested on individual-specific corpora.

	Emergence			**Abstraction**			**Centrality**		
	LEX	SYN	SEM+	*1st/2nd*	*3rd*	*4th*	LOW	MID	HIGH
				Populations-Specific Corpora					
UK	0.61	0.62	0.83	0.81	0.53	0.28	0.83	0.65	0.39
US	0.75	0.69	0.89	0.88	0.64	0.35	0.89	0.74	0.56
				Individual-Specific Corpora					
UK	0.65	0.57	0.76	0.78	0.61	0.41	0.78	0.67	0.50
US	0.70	0.64	0.74	0.78	0.51	0.35	0.77	0.62	0.48

generally higher in the aggregated condition: for instance, the accuracy of SEM+ constructions goes from 0.83 to 0.76 (UK) and from 0.89 to and 0.74 (US). This means that the individual-specific corpora, with noise from both individual differences and social dialects, provide a dialect signal that is less clear. In a few cases (such as with lexical constructions), the situation is changed, with the UK model performing somewhat better in the individual-specific condition. For the best-performing portions of the grammar, however, the aggregated corpora provide a clearer model of dialectal variation. Note that the hierarchy of performance across different nodes of the grammar remains constant. This is important because it means that our conclusions about both the magnitude and the location of dialectal variation in the grammar would be consistent regardless of which type of corpora we observe.

2.5 Summarizing Individual Differences

The analysis in this section has shown that there are more individual differences (i) in more concrete or surface-level constructions and (ii) in more peripheral constructions. This conclusion is reached given two independent families of models, one supervised (classifiers) and one unsupervised (similarity measures). These findings support the usage-based expectation that minor differences in linguistic experience will lead to small differences in the outer edges of the grammar but that those differences will be reduced as constructions are generalized into higher-order representations (becoming more schematic). Having established this, we took a closer look at homogeneity to see that the amount of individual differences present varies by city. We thus conducted a regression analysis which showed a very significant connection between contact with nonlocal populations and higher rates of individual differences. Some members of the population are exposed to these outsiders, leading to diverging linguistic experiences when compared with other members of the population. Factors that increase the diversity of exposure thus increase the amount of individual differences. Importantly, there is no consistent relationship between homogeneity of individuals and homogeneity of aggregated corpora, which means that this effect is a result of individual differences rather than unrelated properties of each local dialect. At the same time, the location of variation within the grammar is consistent regardless of whether we observe individual-specific corpora or aggregated corpora. These findings are important for understanding the source of individual differences in the grammar.

3 Variation across Populations

This third section focuses on dialectal variation: syntactic differences between populations, where *populations* are defined by their geography. We start by presenting the hypothesis that dialectal variation results from repeated iterations of self-exposure within local populations. Put simply, dialects diverge when speakers in one area have more exposure to internal than to external varieties. If this is the case, we would expect that dialects whose speakers have experienced more language contact and population contact should be less distinct. As with individual differences, we begin by measuring the magnitude and robustness of both local and national dialects using a classifier; this framework also allows us to locate where in the grammar dialectal variation exists. We then move to similarity measures, first with a focus on validating them with a classification task and then using them to explore population-based variation in more detail. These studies consider equally both inner-circle and outer-circle dialects: an important advantage of corpus-based methods is that we can apply them equally to under-studied populations.

3.1 Dialect Emergence as Group-Level Exposure

From a usage-based perspective, dialects result from local speech communities which have their own unique sets of exposure. In other words, the emergence of grammar occurs when a discovery-device grammar with minimal starting structures is exposed to particular examples of language use. Each learner is embedded within a specific local community so that they experience more local exposure than nonlocal exposure and thus acquire the local dialect. This approach to variation is generalized in the sense that it ignores social factors like prestige and identity and the strength of ties within a network as direct explanatory variables. For instance, ethnographic work in sociolinguistics has focused on different types of links within small networks, such as weak vs strong ties or hubs vs loners. Such studies operate on networks whose small size is both socially and cognitively unrealistic (Fagyal et al., 2010). And yet if language is a complex system, then scale is essential for studying the emergent properties of language. For instance, more recent empirical work has shown that the effects of these unique types of links disappears as networks approach a realistic size (Laitinen, Fatemi, & Lundberg, 2020). Why would this be the case? Our hypothesis is that local exposure creates dialects and that social relationships like network ties indirectly influence the pattern of exposure.

This means that variation is a side-effect of the emergence of a complex system (the grammar) within a complex network (the population). Previous work has been unable to model complexity effects because it has focused on (i) unrealistically small feature sets and (ii) unrealistically small community networks. Our starting idea here is that exposure influences emergence. A local dialect represents a community that has similar linguistic experience: they communicate with each other. They also communicate with speakers of other dialects and other languages, to differing degrees depending on where they live. For instance, Chicago might have less sustained language contact than Delhi. And London might have more nonlocals than Bristol. Thus, the nature of linguistic experience will differ significantly across these populations.

Dialects with more internal-exposure will be more homogeneous, whereas dialects with more external-exposure will be more heterogeneous; we saw this in Section 2.4. In this context, INTERNAL-EXPOSURE results from communication with other locals while EXTERNAL-EXPOSURE encompasses immigrants and tourists and personal travel. In both cases, exposure could include both face-to-face interactions, digital interactions, and (social) media consumption. While previous work has often assumed that exposure to variants takes place during face-to-face interactions only, the prevalence and importance of digital communication for most people calls such an assumption into question.

Previous work has been limited by methodology to small-scale situations: miniature social networks and arbitrary, isolated features. As a result, the importance of individual relationships and social evaluations, like prestige, has likely been overstated. Our methods here take the corrective of focusing only on exposure. For instance, immigrant populations are largely low-prestige. Thus, traditionally they would have little impact on dialectal variation. Here we can undertake a natural experiment to see whether this is actually the case: what impacts do immigrants have? If there is a systematic influence from the contact situations such populations create, then social evaluations like prestige alone are inadequate. By not including social factors in the models we can determine how much variation can be explained by exposure on its own.

How would we know if a model with only access to exposure is sufficient for modeling dialectal variation? The approach in this Element uses both classifiers (supervised) and similarity measures (unsupervised) to model syntactic differences across distinct portions of the grammar. Both of these models are validated using prediction accuracy: how well they are able to distinguish between individuals or between local dialects or between national dialects or between registers. A high accuracy means that the model is able to reliably distinguish between, say, Midwestern American English and West Coast American English. In short, if we can build a model to predict dialectal production than we have captured *how* dialectal grammars work and if we can build a model to predict which dialects are more similar than we have captured *why* dialectal grammars exist in the first place.

If these models, with access to exposure but not to social factors, are able to adequately model variation along these dimensions, then this indicates that the importance of social factors has been unfortunately magnified in the existing literature as a side-effect of relying on unnaturally small samples of both the grammar and the population. To be clear, the argument here is not that social factors like prestige and identity are not involved in variation and diffusion. The argument, however, is that the importance of these factors has been overestimated because of a reliance on small-scale studies: small snippets of the grammar used by small parts of the population in limited registers. Language is a complex system and the speech community is a complex system. The essential problem is that emergent effects of complex systems cannot be observed within isolated snippets of those systems.

3.2 Magnitude and Robustness: How Much Dialectal Variation?

We begin by measuring the magnitude and robustness of national dialects using the same classification-based approach that we used for individual-level variation. The goal, as before, is to determine both how much syntactic dialectal variation there is in written registers and also where exactly it is located in the grammar. This section works with both local and national dialects. For the first task, we include fourteen countries, as shown in Table 9; this experiment uses a single classifier that includes both inner-circle and outer-circle varieties. For the second task, we distinguish between regional dialects within the same area: for example, Midwestern American English and Western Canadian English are included in a single classifier for North American regional dialects.

Table 9 Classification accuracy for national dialects as measured by the f-score. Accuracy is estimated over ten unique rounds, with each round using one region to represent the national dialects. For example, the Perth region might represent Australian English in one round and the Sydney region in another. The min and max values are estimated using a Bayesian confidence interval of 95% across five-fold cross-validation within each round. All values are significantly higher than the majority baseline.

	Level of Abstraction					
	First-Order		**Third-Order**		**Fourth-Order**	
	Min	*Max*	*Min*	*Max*	*Min*	*Max*
All Countries	0.94	0.95	0.74	0.75	0.47	0.48
	Order of Emergence					
	LEX		SYN		SEM+	
	Min	*Max*	*Min*	*Max*	*Min*	*Max*
All Countries	0.87	0.87	0.80	0.82	0.95	0.95
	Degree of Centrality					
	Low		**Mid**		**High**	
	Min	*Max*	*Min*	*Max*	*Min*	*Max*
All Countries	0.93	0.94	0.87	0.88	0.66	0.67

As before, we estimate classification performance across two layers: first, we use ten rounds of classification, each with a unique set of regions. Thus, rather than mix samples from Perth and Sydney together in a representation of Australian English, each round represents the national dialect using only a single local area within that dialect. This allows us to determine robustness of national dialects across local areas. Then, within each such round, we use five-fold cross-validation to ensure we are not over-fitting a specific test set. Table 9 reports the minimum and maximum values for the f-score at a 95% confidence interval. The magnitude of variation is represented by the f-score (higher scores indicate more variation) and the robustness by the range between the min and max values: a less robust model will show more variation across these specific classification instances.

First, in terms of magnitude, some parts of the grammar are able to distinguish national dialects quite clearly: the top scores are between 0.94 and 0.95 (first-order constructions) and 0.95 (the late-stage SEM+ constructions which contain several word classes and have access to nonlocal occurrence information). As before, a high accuracy means that there is more variation available to distinguish samples from different dialects. Thus, this means that there is significant syntactic variation across national dialects in written registers. Further, the range between the minimum and maximum scores is generally within a single point (e.g., 0.74 vs 0.75). This means that variation is consistent; because of the rigorous experimental design, we can have high confidence that these are valid estimates of the amount of variation present in the grammar.

But where exactly is that variation located? As with individual variation, by level of abstraction there is much more variation in lower-level concrete first-order and second-order constructions (0.94–0.95). Likewise, there is a clear and significant downward trend in variation as constructions become more abstract: down to 0.74 minimum for third-order constructions and then down to 0.47 minimum for fourth-order constructions. This means, for instance, that there is much less difference across national dialects in the usage of these abstract representations.

Within degree of centrality, we see a much stronger version of the same pattern as individual variation: most variation is concentrated in peripheral constructions. The magnitude of this difference is much greater here, however, with a relatively low minimum f-score of 0.66 in the core grammar (HIGH) and a relatively high minimum f-score of 0.93 in the periphery of the grammar (LOW). This means that variation is concentrated in lightly entrenched constructions.

Finally, by order of emergence, the location of variation differs strikingly from the location of individual differences. For individual differences in the classification experiment, there was no significant difference along order of emergence; in the unsupervised similarity measures, there was a slight difference with early-stage lexical constructions subject to more variation. For national dialects this is reversed: there are strong and significant differences by order of emergence, with most variation concentrated in the late-stage constructions (SEM+). Interestingly, there is more variation in early-stage lexical constructions than in middle-stage constructions. This means that individual differences are not structured around the order of emergence of constructions while dialectal differences are concentrated in late-stage constructions.

In order to get a more detailed picture of dialect variation, we show the f-score across level of abstractness for each national dialect in Table 10. Although there is a single model for all dialects, inner-circle dialects are shown at the top and outer-circle at the bottom. The *Support* columns shows the average number of test samples per round. This table allows us to see, for instance,

Table 10 Average f-score for specific national dialects across level of abstractness. All dialects are contained in a single model but divided into inner-circle and outer-circle groups for convenience. The average f-score per country is calculated across ten rounds, each with a distinct inventory of regions included to provide an estimate of the robustness across specific local areas.

Inner-Circle Dialects by Abstractness				
Country	**First-Order**	**Third-Order**	**Fourth-Order**	**Support**
AU	0.92	0.41	0.26	4,307
CA	0.97	0.64	0.32	4,749
IE	0.95	0.73	0.45	5,628
NZ	0.91	0.57	0.34	5,622
UK	0.89	0.60	0.20	4,945
US	0.97	0.79	0.47	5,305
Outer-Circle Dialects by Abstractness				
Country	**First-Order**	**Third-Order**	**Fourth-Order**	**Support**
BD	0.90	0.77	0.51	4,829
ID	0.88	0.71	0.40	5,653
IN	0.98	0.90	0.74	4,265
KE	1.00	0.86	0.61	4,348
MY	0.93	0.76	0.41	3,589
NG	0.99	0.89	0.61	5,561
PH	0.96	0.76	0.43	4,060
PK	0.92	0.84	0.67	5,612

that all dialects have the same hierarchy (with more variation at lower levels of abstraction) even though there is considerable difference in the uniqueness of each dialect.

Outer-circle dialects tend to be more unique (i.e., to have more variation that distinguishes them from other dialects), a trend that continues at each level of abstraction. This is expected if we view dialect to be a result of exposure: outer-circle dialects in general experience more language contact. Thus, outer-circle dialects are each exposed to a unique set of other languages; the local languages for Indian English are quite different from the local language for Nigerian English and this shows in their relative uniqueness. Further, exposure is asymmetrical, with outer-circle varieties having much contact with inner-circle varieties but not vice-versa. If dialectal variation is driven mostly by exposure, then these kinds of increased exposure to other languages and other dialects will create more variation within outer-circle dialects.

Within inner-circle varieties, the classification accuracy for the most abstract fourth-order constructions is quite low: ranging from 0.20 to 0.34 to 0.47 at the highest. This means that, in their usage of abstract constructions, these dialects largely agree and thus are difficult to tell apart. Within outer-circle varieties, accuracy is much higher even within the most abstract constructions, as high as 0.74 (India) and 0.67 (Pakistan). This means that there is variation even in the most abstract regions of the grammar. If we view syntax as a lexico-syntactic continuum, with some constructions more lexical and others more syntactic, this means that outer-circle varieties have deeper syntactic differences than do inner-circle varieties.

Moving from national to local dialects, we take a finer grain-size by focusing on local dialects within the same region: for example, Midwestern American English vs East Coast American English, both within a single North American model. This is shown in Table 11 with each division of the grammar across six areas. As before, we estimate classification accuracy using ten rounds, each with a random sample of local areas from the same region. This classifier is limited to six local dialects so that more regions can be included. This means that, while we can compare magnitude across areas, we cannot directly compare magnitude with the national dialects, which had an inventory of fourteen dialects. Classification performance in Table 11 is shown by region: *Africa* contains Kenya and Nigeria; *Europe* contains the UK and Ireland; *North America* contains the US and Canada; *Oceania* contains Australia and New Zealand; *South Asia* contains India, Pakistan, and Bangladesh; *Southeast Asia* contains Malaysia, the Philippines, and Indonesia.

As noted above, having fewer classes makes the classification task easier. The majority baseline in this set-up for national dialects is 7.1% accuracy, while it is 16.6% accuracy here. In spite of this higher majority baseline, the classification scores are much lower which indicates that there is much less syntactic variation between local dialects from the same area. For instance, the highest f-score for first-order constructions is 0.85 minimum (North America) and the lowest is 0.75 minimum (Africa and Oceania). Interestingly, there is no clear distinction between inner-circle and outer-circle dialects in terms of the magnitude or robustness of variation. The basic conclusion is that local dialects have significantly more variation than the baseline but significantly less than national dialects.

But where in the grammar are the differences between local dialects concentrated? As before, the least abstract constructions (first-order) have the most variation by level of abstraction. And the late-stage constructions (SEM+) have

Table 11 Classification accuracy for local dialects as represented by the f-score for classifying local areas within the same region. For consistency across regions, each classifier includes six local areas. Classification is repeated across ten rounds, each with a unique subset of local areas. Regions are represented by the mean across test samples within that region. All values are significantly higher than the majority baseline.

	Level of Abstraction					
	First-Order		**Third-Order**		**Fourth-Order**	
	Min	*Max*	*Min*	*Max*	*Min*	*Max*
Africa	0.75	0.75	0.56	0.56	0.43	0.43
Europe	0.79	0.79	0.48	0.48	0.30	0.30
North America	0.85	0.86	0.57	0.59	0.35	0.36
Oceania	0.75	0.76	0.40	0.41	0.28	0.29
South Asia	0.82	0.85	0.64	0.66	0.49	0.52
Southeast Asia	0.81	0.81	0.59	0.60	0.40	0.40
	Order of Emergence					
	LEX		SYN		SEM+	
	Min	*Max*	*Min*	*Max*	*Min*	*Max*
Africa	0.68	0.68	0.61	0.61	0.74	0.74
Europe	0.60	0.60	0.58	0.58	0.77	0.77
North America	0.67	0.70	0.59	0.60	0.83	0.85
Oceania	0.54	0.56	0.54	0.55	0.71	0.72
South Asia	0.74	0.76	0.66	0.69	0.81	0.83
Southeast Asia	0.73	0.74	0.62	0.63	0.80	0.81
	Degree of Centrality					
	Low		**Mid**		**High**	
	Min	*Max*	*Min*	*Max*	*Min*	*Max*
Africa	0.74	0.74	0.64	0.64	0.52	0.52
Europe	0.76	0.77	0.63	0.64	0.43	0.44
North America	0.84	0.86	0.65	0.67	0.48	0.50
Oceania	0.72	0.73	0.59	0.60	0.35	0.36
South Asia	0.79	0.81	0.72	0.75	0.61	0.64
Southeast Asia	0.80	0.81	0.72	0.73	0.55	0.56

the most variation by order of emergence. And constructions on the periphery (LOW) have much more variation than constructions in the core of the grammar (HIGH). Thus, the pattern of variation within the grammar is the same as with national dialects, simply at a lower magnitude.

This section has explored the magnitude and robustness and location of dialectal variation at both the national and the local level. While national dialects have much more variation, there is still a significant amount of syntactic difference between regional dialects (like Midwestern American English) in written corpora. In both cases, that variation is concentrated in less abstract and peripheral constructions that emerge in the later stages of grammar learning. This contrasts to some degree with individual differences, which have more variation in early lexical representations than in later representations.

3.3 Evaluating Local and National Similarity Measures

This section continues our investigation of national and local dialects using unsupervised similarity measures. The methodology behind these measures is explained above in the section on individual differences: each comparison (i.e., Australian vs New Zealand English) is estimated by sampling 1,000 pairs of samples from the underlying populations. We use cosine distance over standardized token frequencies, with classification weights used to focus on salient constructions. The resulting similarity measures are standardized across the entire dataset so that we can interpret which distances are comparatively large and which are comparatively small. Because we are using standardized cosine distance, a value of 0 indicates that the difference is average, a value of 1.0 means the distance is one standard deviation greater than the mean (i.e., more different), and a value of −1.0 means the distance is one standard deviation below the mean (i.e., more similar).

We start by validating the similarity measures using a classification task: are samples from the same local dialect more similar to one another than to samples from other local dialects? This is shown in Table 12, aggregated by country. Each local dialect is compared with other local dialects within the same region; thus, Christchurch would be compared with Dunedin but not with Chicago. This focus on local dialects makes the task more difficult and tests the ability of these unsupervised measures to make precise distinctions based on constructional features. We estimate the minimum and maximum range of similarity between local dialects using a Bayesian estimate with a 95% confidence interval; a correct classification occurs when there is no overlap between same-city and different-city measures. The aggregations in Table 12 show the

Table 12 Accuracy of unsupervised similarity measures for categorizing local dialects. Measure in accuracy (percent correct). A correct categorization makes samples from a local dialect (like Chicago) more similar to one another than to other dialects from the same region. Results are aggregated by country.

	Emergence			Abstraction			Centrality		
	LEX	SYN	FULL	*1st/2nd*	*3rd*	*4th*	LOW	MID	HIGH
AU	100	99.8	100	90.3	71.2	99.8	98.0	79.1	99.5
CA	100	99.9	99.0	97.9	61.3	97.2	99.7	72.4	96.3
IE	100	99.8	100	99.3	67.5	100	99.8	79.9	100
NZ	100	99.8	100	89.8	67.5	99.6	97.1	73.8	99.4
UK	99.9	99.7	100	95.0	60.8	97.3	99.5	73.9	99.7
US	99.3	98.1	99.3	99.8	52.9	95.9	100	75.9	99.7
BD	99.8	97.8	99.8	96.7	78.9	93.2	99.3	80.0	96.7
ID	99.6	98.7	99.4	95.9	88.1	83.6	98.1	91.1	89.3
IN	99.7	96.1	97.1	97.0	94.3	98.8	98.4	95.2	99.3
KE	99.3	99.8	99.4	97.4	92.7	99.6	98.9	99.4	100
MY	98.0	97.7	98.2	96.5	77.9	96.4	98.4	81.4	98.8
NG	100	99.9	100	97.1	78.5	99.8	99.1	83.1	99.9
PH	99.5	99.0	99.9	96.7	74.5	97.7	98.5	84.5	99.0
PK	99.8	98.4	98.8	93.7	94.2	98.2	97.7	95.9	99.5

average accuracy by country; the complete city-by-city results are available in the supplementary material.

Our first question here is about the validity of this unsupervised approach to dialectal variation. The results are quite high across countries; for instance, the accuracy of first-order constructions ranges from 90.3% (Australia) to 99.8% (US). This means that the similarity measures can detect even subtle differences between local city-based dialects. This high accuracy justifies our use of these measures to further explore dialectal variation in the next section.

Our second question is about where variation is located in the grammar. This particular design allows us to test the validity of the measures, but offers less insight into the particular distribution of varying constructions. This is because we are testing for a significant difference between the estimated average distance, whereas the classifier experiments above were making predictions about each sample. We can also see that many parts of the grammar reach a ceiling of high performance in Table 12: most columns are above 90% accuracy on average.

This section has shown that similarity measures are robustly accurate for distinguishing local dialects. Importantly, the location of dialectal variation within the grammar is quite similar regardless of the family of model we use to uncover that variation, whether supervised or unsupervised. This converging evidence replicates the main findings. Additional analysis of the validity of similarity measures in this setting is available in the supplementary materials.[6] Given that both models are accurate and converge in their depictions of dialectal variation, we now proceed with a deeper examination of dialectal syntax.

3.4 Exploring Dialectal Differences

We begin this section with an analysis of how syntactic variation is organized across the population; while the previous analysis looked at where variants were located within the grammar, here we focus on how similar national and regional dialects are. The similarity measures are highly accurate, thus validating their use for understanding dialectal variation.

We start with a clustermap which shows the estimated similarity between national dialects together with a denrogram representing a hierarchical clustering of dialects in Figure 7. The estimated similarity is drawn from 1,000 pairwise similarities between each city-level dialect. The similarity between Australia and New Zealand, then, is the average similarity across all pairs of individual cities. As shown in Table 12, this approach provides estimates of similarity that are both accurate and robust. The underlying heatmap shows the distance between national dialects; darker blue colors indicate a low distance (c.f., the diagonal) while darker red colors indicate a higher distance (e.g., India and the US). The arrangement of the heatmap follows the results of hierarchical clustering, shown by the tree diagram on the left of the figure. Clusters that are further apart indicate larger differences. This is an entirely unsupervised pipeline so that the population structure is based on syntactic structures alone.

The first cluster, as expected, separates outer-circle dialects (at the top) from inner-circle dialects (at the bottom). Of more interest is the structure within each of these clusters. The dialects are grouped into regions and this is reflected in the subclusters of outer-circle varieties: African English (NG, KE), South Asian Englishes (BD, IN, PK), and Southeast Asian Englishes (ID, PH, MY). Within inner-circle varieties, we see a similar organization: European dialects (UK, IE), to which NZ is added, with AU as the last member, closest to NZ. This branch is distinguished from the US and CA at the bottom. Thus, from a syntactic perspective Commonwealth dialects are distinct from North

[6] https://doi.org/10.17605/OSF.IO/A57US.

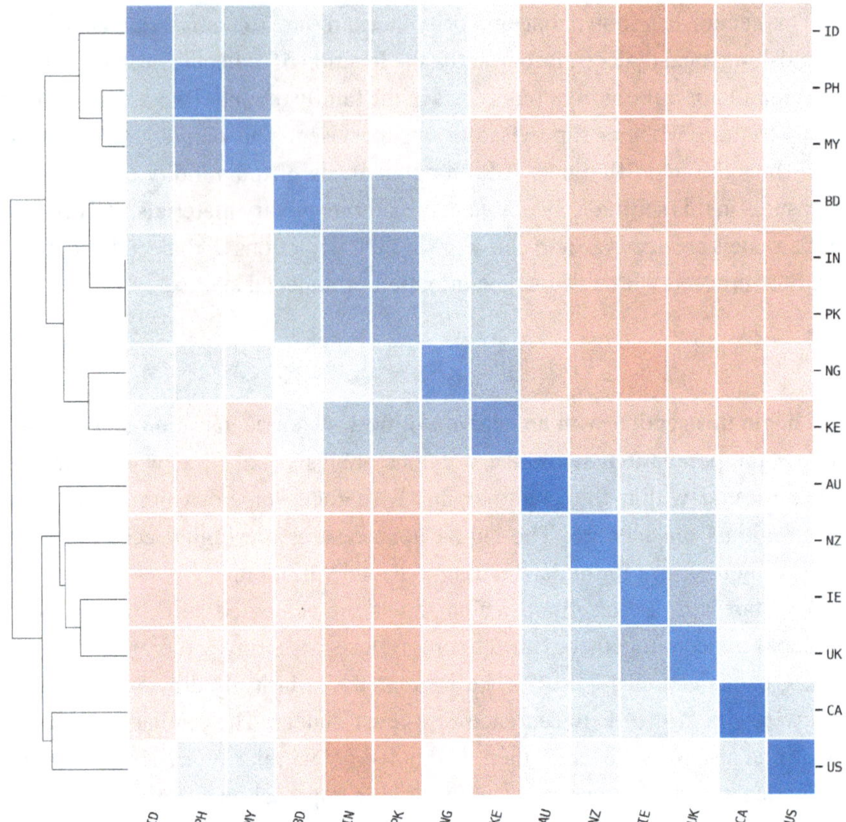

Figure 7 Clustermap of national dialects with late-stage (SEM+) constructions. This is an entirely unsupervised taxonomy.

American dialects. New Zealand is positioned interestingly between European and Australian English. Thus, this figure shows that unsupervised similarity measures are able to reconstruct population-based similarities using only syntactic representations. This figure visualizes similarities within the late-stage grammar (SEM+); figures for other parts of the grammar are available in the supplementary material.

We take a closer look at regional dialects in North America in Figure 8. Each region is a collection of city-level dialects; the name of the city with the most samples in each region is given as an illustration of the location of the region. As expected, the first major division among North American regional dialects is between American (bottom) and Canadian English (top). The outlier within Canadian English is Montreal (region CA-3). Within American English, there is a southern cluster exemplified by Atlanta (US-4) and Houston (US-3). This is part of a larger southern and western cluster, together with Phoenix (US-6) and Long Beach (US-9). Consulting the map of regions shown

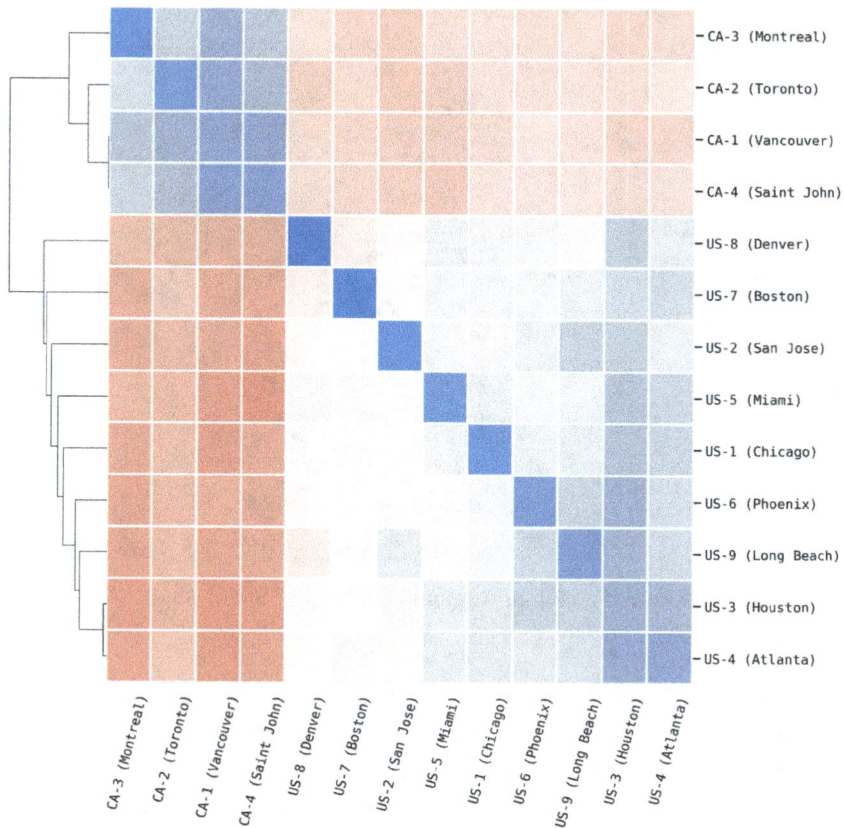

Figure 8 Clustermap of regional dialects within North America with late-stage (SEM+) constructions. This is an entirely unsupervised taxonomy.

previously in Figure 2, this larger cluster contains dialect areas in the southern portion of the US from east to west. The exception is Miami (US-5) which is in fact more similar to Chicago (US-1). This raises an important question about the structure of American dialects: here we see influence from both geography and the historical east-to-west colonization of the US, but also from more recent immigration and the language contact it has caused. The scale of a computational corpus-based approach to variation is important for untangling these factors.

This can be contrasted with regional dialects in South Asia, where patterns of political boundaries and language contact are quite different. For reference, a map of regional dialects in South Asia (India, Pakistan, and Bangladesh) is shown in Figure 9; each point is a city and cities of the same color make up a regional dialect. The clustermap of regional dialects is shown in Figure 10. Here there is more difference within India, between southern regions in cities like Chennai (IN-8) and northern regions in cities like Delhi (IN-1). The

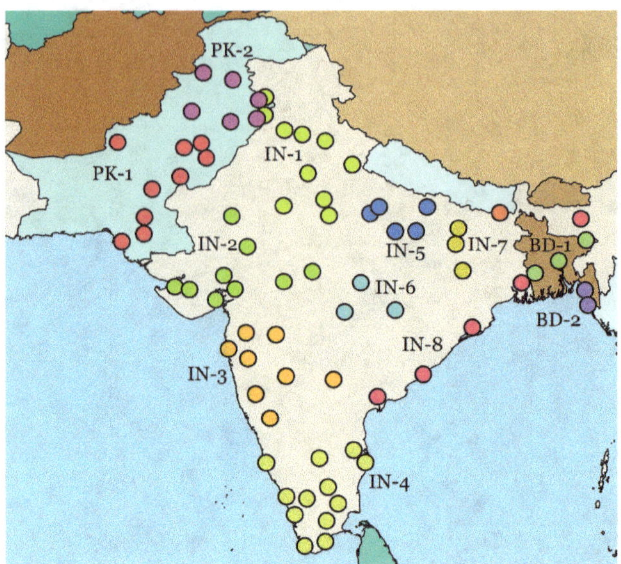

Figure 9 Map of Regional Dialects in South Asia.

regional dialects from Pakistan and Bangladesh still cluster together, put some Indian cities like Ranchi are much less similar to other Indian cities. Similarity measures are important here because a classification approach would assume boundaries rather than construct them. These similarity results show, then, the syntactic variation mirrors underlying differences in the population, differences which cause syntactic variation. This is explored further below.

Stepping back briefly, to what degree would clusters like those shown in Figure 7 be stable across different portions of the grammar? In other words, part of our goal is to understand how social factors cause syntactic variation. The problem with most existing work is scale, in that the focus is on discrete alternations (variables) in isolation. We thus investigate whether similarity relationships between national dialects are consistent across parts of the grammar in Figure 11. This heatmap shows Spearman correlations between similarity ranks, so that high values (like within order of emergence) mean that the part of the grammar we observe has no influence while low values (like by degree of centrality) mean that the part of the grammar we observe has a large influence. This is also a view of how diffusion takes place throughout the grammar, with synchronic similarity reflecting diachronic processes of diffusion.

First, we see that order of emergence (the upper-left square) is consistent: similarity ranks do not change. For level of abstraction (the center squares), we see that fourth-order constructions differ from first/second-order and third-order constructions. For degree of centrality (bottom-right square), core

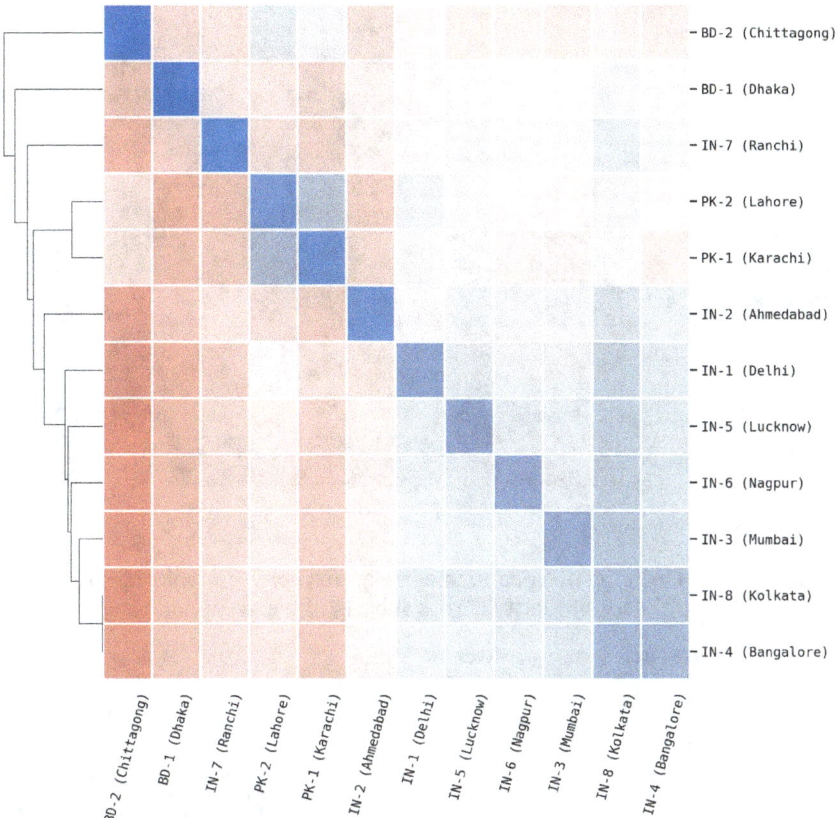

Figure 10 Clustermap of regional dialects within South Asia with late-stage (SEM+) constructions. This is an entirely unsupervised taxonomy.

constructions have almost no relationship at all to constructions more on the periphery (low and mid). This is not a repetition of the finding we have seen before, that the accuracy of the measures has this same pattern, but it is a related observation. What this means is that we would come away with a very different view of syntactic variation if we looked at highly abstract vs concrete constructions or core vs peripheral constructions. This is important because it means that the complex network structure of the grammar has a role in syntactic variation and its diffusion. It also means that work which relies on a small number of hand-crafted features essentially observes an arbitrary subset of the overall syntactic variation.

The analysis so far has worked with estimated similarities between dialects which are sampled from a larger population of observed pairwise similarities. In Figure 12 we visualize this as a violin plot showing the full distribution instead. Each comparison involves observing 1,000 pairs of samples. Here we are looking at self-similarity or homogeneity in which each city is compared

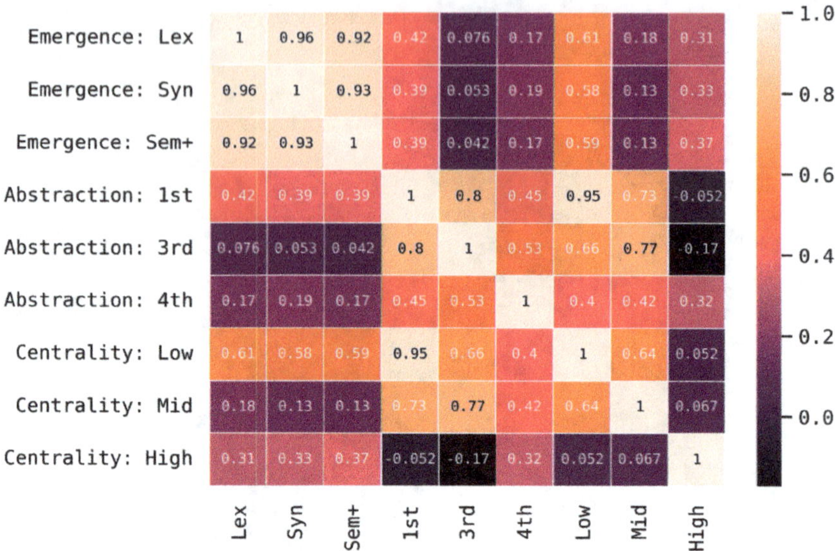

Figure 11 Heatmap of Spearman correlations between ranks of national dialect similarity across subsets of the grammar.

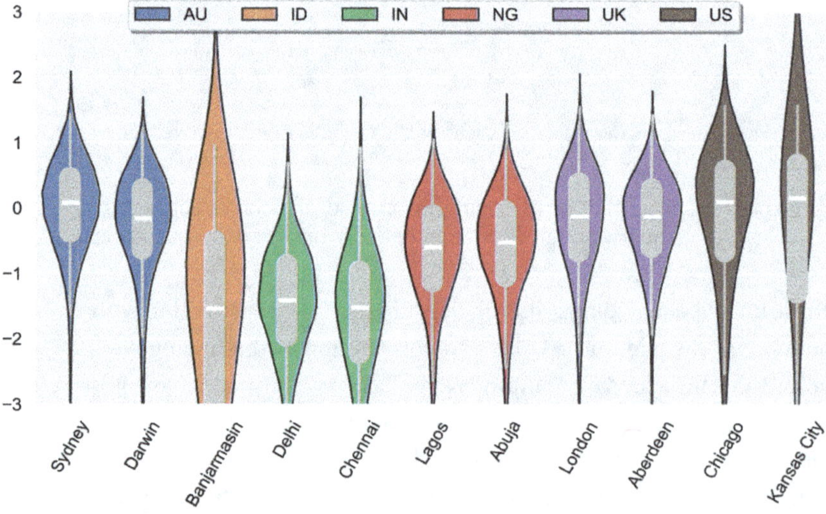

Figure 12 Homogeneity at the city level across countries with first-order constructions.

with other samples from the same city. This differs from the analysis in Figure 4 because the samples are aggregated, not representing single individuals. As before, we first standardize across the entire set of comparisons in order to determine what a high or low similarity looks like. Then we visualize comparisons within cities in this standardized space. The figure shows two cities each from six countries, half inner-circle and half outer-circle.

The estimated similarity is the mean of this distribution, indicated here by the horizontal white line within each violin plot. The widest point within each violin indicates more samples falling in that range; thus, outliers are represented by very slender lines extending from the main distribution. This is based on cosine distance, which means that higher values (like Sydney) are less self-similar and lower values (like Chennai) are more self-similar. A compact distribution (like Darwin) means that the 1,000 pairs all fall into the same range; a stretched distribution (like Kansas City) means that there is much variance within the city.

This figure shows that countries and even cities within countries differ in their level of homogeneity. Some places, like Kansas City, show a range of behaviours while others are more narrowly constrained. All self-comparisons have relatively high similarity (falling below the mean), so that these populations are more coherent than even regional dialects. But the range of that coherence varies. We have seen that homogeneity in individual-specific corpora, which represents individual differences within a city, are best predicted by the amount of population contact with distant communities: places with more outside contact have more individual differences. For population-specific corpora, though, the samples are aggregated across unknown individuals already; thus, homogeneity here is not a reflection of more individual differences. This was shown in Figure 6, where homogeneity by city is not consistently correlated between population-based and individual-based corpora. So what exactly does homogeneity in these aggregated samples reflect? It has to do with the relative importance of geographic variation in a place over individual and social variation. A more homogeneous city means that geographic variation is more important than other sources of variation.

So far we have seen that (i) unsupervised similarity measures are highly accurate for identifying same-dialect vs different-dialect samples and (ii) that clusters of samples based on these similarity measures correspond with historic relationships between dialects. But the advantage of a computational approach is that we can go beyond a hierarchy of dialects and look at explanatory factors. Here we do this using a linear mixed effects model. Our dependent variable is the estimated similarity between cities belonging to distinct regional (i.e., Midwest American English vs East Coast American English), national (i.e., American vs Nigerian English), and circle-level (inner vs outer) groups. Given the large corpora we are working with, this means we have 46,665 observed pairs of cities. Each pair has an estimated syntactic similarity, based on a specific part of the grammar. The goal of the regression analysis is to determine what explanatory factors make dialects more or less similar as a way of understanding the mechanisms of language variation and change.

As with our regression to understand individual differences, we draw on several external factors dealing with population contact and linguistic diversity. First, we use estimated air travel between cities as a proxy for the amount of contact between two places (Huang et al., 2013); more air travel reflects more communication in general. Second, we use the geographic distance between cities as a second measure of contact: cities that are close together will also have more exposure to their respective dialects.

Third, we use the digital linguistic landscape, from social media, to quantify the difference in language contact situations experienced by the two cities. Since we are observing a specific population of Twitter users, we estimate the share of languages used in each city and take the cosine distance between shares; for instance, in Montreal 49% of digital language is French while in Toronto the share of French is only 0.8%. This means the two cities differ greatly in the language contact they are experiencing. Since English predominates in digital spaces, we split this into two variables: agreement overall in linguistic landscape (using the cosine distance of language shares) and agreement without English considered. Fourth, we include two categorical variables: whether the two cities are located in the same country and within the same circle (outer vs inner).

Finally, we include the first city as a random effect to control for variations at the city level, much like viewing each city's population as a unique participant. This regression model allows us to see to what degree similarity overall can be explained by variables representing the amount of external exposure and language contact in each pair being considered. In other words, we are testing whether more similar linguistic experiences lead to more similar dialects.

The coefficients of significant variables for the model specific to each portion of the grammar are shown in Table 13 (significance is defined here as $p < 0.001$). All models converge and most factors are significant for most parts of the grammar; travel as a proxy for exposure is the most likely to not be a significant predictor variable. Because the model is predicting a distance measure, positive coefficients mean that a factor makes two dialects more different and negative coefficients mean that a factor makes two dialects more similar. Our first observation from this table is that we would get a different view of which factors are significant depending on which part of the grammar we observe; this calls into questions studies which rely on a small number of constructions for their conclusions (c.f., Szmrecsanyi, Grafmiller, & Rosseel 2019). For instance, there is less variation in more abstract and more core constructions, and as a result the explanatory value of factors given these parts of the grammar is generally lower.

Table 13 Coefficients of significant values from a Linear Mixed Effects model with city as a random effect and explanatory variables (shown in the table) as fixed effects. Positive coefficients make two cities more different and negative coefficients make them more similar. All models converge and all shown coefficients are significant at the $p < 0.001$ level.

	Level of Abstraction		
	First	*Third*	*Fourth*
Country (Same)	−0.37	−0.07	ns
Circle (Same)	−0.21	−0.12	−0.04
Landscape (All)	−0.49	−0.40	0.07
Landscape (Non-ENG)	−0.23	−0.34	−0.07
Exposure (Travel)	ns	ns	ns
Exposure (KMs)	0.00	0.00	0.00
	Order of Emergence		
	LEX	SYN	SEM+
Country (Same)	−0.47	−0.66	−0.67
Circle (Same)	−0.35	−0.45	−0.43
Landscape (All)	−0.18	−0.30	−0.30
Landscape (Non-ENG)	0.20	0.33	0.28
Exposure (Travel)	ns	0.00	0.00
Exposure (KMs)	0.00	0.00	0.00
	Degree of Centrality		
	Low	*Mid*	*High*
Country (Same)	−0.38	−0.24	−0.02
Circle (Same)	−0.22	−0.14	−0.03
Landscape (All)	−0.40	−0.14	0.13
Landscape (Non−ENG)	−0.09	−0.34	0.08
Exposure (Travel)	ns	0.00	0.00
Exposure (KMs)	0.00	0.00	0.00

The strongest predictor variables are about linguistic landscape: cities with a similar mix of languages being used in digital contexts are more similar syntactically. The variables reflecting exposure (as approximated by the amount of travel and the geographic distance) are significant in most cases but also have very low coefficients and thus little impact on the model. It remains the case, though, that cities from the same country and from the same circle are much more likely to be similar. These last two variables partly represent increased exposure but also serve as a validation of the model: of course we expect that different cities within the US to be more similar with each other than with cities from Nigeria. The take-away from this model is that language contact has a surprising influence on the syntactic similarity of dialects.

Previously, in the regression to understand why some cities have more individual differences than others, the amount of incoming travel from other countries (exposure) was more of a factor than language contact. Thus, here we are seeing a difference in causal factors between individual and group-level differences. Individual differences and dialect variation are located in mostly the same portion of the grammar. They also result from differences in exposure to outside populations. Short-term exposure, however, is more likely to be represented by air traffic (because it includes tourists and business travelers), while long-term exposure is more likely to be represented by the digital linguistic landscape (because immigrants and students will alter that landscape). We thus see a nuanced distinction between the kinds of exposure which a population is experiencing. Dialects are more influenced by long-term exposure.

We visualize the residual errors of this analysis for the late-stage SEM+ constructions in Figure 13. The red line in the center reflects cases where the explanatory variables exactly predict the level of syntactic similarity between

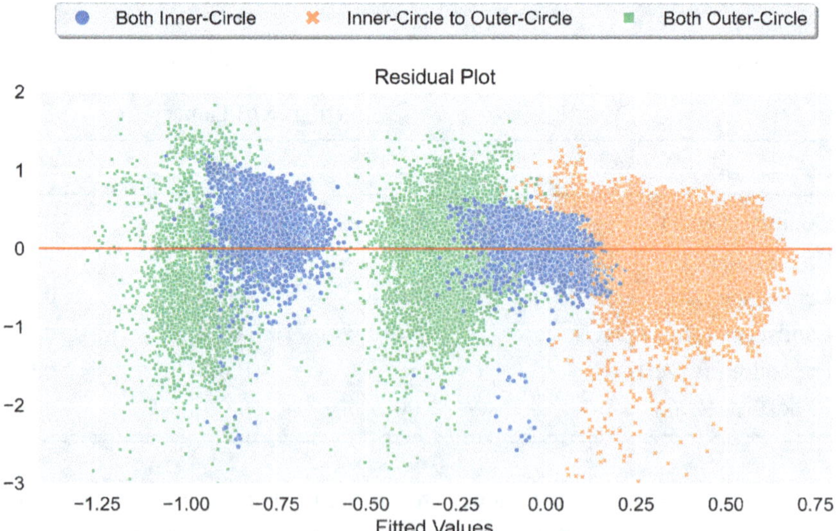

Figure 13 Residual errors for the regression analysis of factors explaining the similarity of city-level dialects using late-stage SEM+ features. High values indicate that pairs are predicted to be more different than they are and low values indicate that pairs are predicted to be more similar than they actually are.

two cities. Errors are indicated by the distance of points above the line (if the prediction is more different than actually observed) and below the line (if the prediction is more similar than actually observed). Pairs are separated by color into three categories: both cities are inner-circle, both cities are outer-circle, or the comparison crosses from inner to outer-circles. Most points are relatively close to the predicted line. Note that this scatterplot contains 46,665 points so that the densest regions are overlapping and thus underestimated visually.

Most outlying samples are predicted to be more similar than they actually are. Further, most outliers are pairs of outer-circle dialects (the reddish squares). A fair number of outliers are pairs that cross between inner-circle and outer-circle. Very few inner-circle pairs are outliers. This means that the factors which influence syntactic similarity are somewhat different in outer-circle contexts, so that the model's predicted similarities are less accurate. The model does take into account the linguistic landscape, and outer-circle varieties are subject generally to much more language contact than inner-circle varieties. Thus, language contact itself is not likely to be the cause here. Outer-circle speakers are more likely to be bilingual speakers, perhaps with English as their second language, but again this would be captured by the landscape variable and the random effect by city. A cause that is not taken into account here is the asymmetric nature of exposure: outer-circle populations are exposed to and aware of inner-circle populations, but not vice-versa. For instance, media is more likely to conform to inner-circle standards and language technology (important for digital communication) almost uniformly performs much better for inner-circle dialects. The missing factor, then, is likely to be about the directionality of exposure.

For a concluding analysis of dialectal variation, we now view local cities as nodes in a network which are connected by our syntactic distances as edge weights. Thus, if two cities are similar, this is described using their edge weight. Viewed in this way, we can determine if some local dialects are *loners*, with only distant connections to all other dialects and others are *hubs*, with close connections to many other dialects. This is analyzed at the city-level; thus, this network has 304 nodes and over 46k edges. As before, we are also interested in complexity within the grammar; for this reason we create a separate network for each of the portions of the grammar we have been analyzing, by order of emergence and level of abstraction and degree of centrality. This network-based analysis will allow us to examine whether exposure can be asymmetric, with some regions acting as connecting hubs.

We measure the centrality of cities within this network using Eigenvector Centrality, an approach which accounts for the centrality of nearby cities as

Table 14 The most central (left) and most peripheral (right) local dialects as measured using Eigenvalue Centrality in the network derived from late-stage (SEM+) constructions.

Top 10 Most Central Regions			**Bottom 10 Least Central Regions**		
Region	*Example*	*Centrality*	*Region*	*Example*	*Centrality*
IE-1	Dublin	1.953	PH-2	Davao	−0.860
UK-5	Belfast	1.851	IN-2	Ahmedabad	−0.870
UK-3	Glasgow	1.804	IN-7	Ranchi	−0.881
UK-1	London	1.664	IN-3	Mumbai	−1.031
UK-4	Leeds	1.590	IN-1	Delhi	−1.038
UK-2	Birmingham	1.553	ID-2	Medan	−1.067
NZ-2	Wellington	1.483	IN-6	Nagpur	−1.078
AU-2	Sydney	1.359	IN-4	Bangalore	−1.097
AU-3	Melbourne	1.355	IN-5	Lucknow	−1.196
NZ-1	Auckland	1.322	IN-8	Kolkata	−1.397

well. Thus, with a colonial example, if a city like Sydney has certain similarities to London, which is itself highly central, the centrality of Sydney will be increased. We take the mean centrality by region in Table 14 with the late-stage SEM+ network. This table is arranged with the most central regional dialects on the left and the most peripheral on the right. The centrality measure here is standardized so that 1 indicates one standard deviation above the mean and -1 one standard deviation below the mean.

We notice from this figure that there is a clear distinction between inner-circle and outer-circle dialects: the most central regions are all inner-circle and least central are all outer-circle. Within the most central dialects, all are varieties of British or Irish English. From a historical perspective, this is an accurate reflection of colonial patterns even though it is derived from synchronic similarity measures with no geographic or social information. Since dialects from the UK are quite central, any dialect which is itself similar to that central hub will also be more central; thus, commonwealth dialects like Australian and New Zealand English are more central than American English (c.f., the clusters of similar dialects in Figure 7. Note, also, that the definition of centrality takes into account influence among outer-circle dialects as well because this is a global network. Thus, an inner-circle dialect with more connections with and influence over outer-circle dialects will be more central. The complete ranking of centrality by regional dialect across nodes of the grammar is available in the supplementary material.

This network view of dialect similarity is important because it adds a dimension which the previous regression analysis ignored by viewing the network as a simple set of pairs. The network of dialects of English is actually a set of nodes. For instance, UK English is a central dialect; even if other dialects are more similar to each other (i.e., Indian English to Pakistani English), the hub is composed of those dialects which are most closely connected to all other branches. In this case, the branches result from historical patterns of colonization and resulting language contact. This tells us that (i) historic sources of exposure create variations which remain visible far in the future, and (ii) exposure can be asymmetrical. In other words, our previous analysis looked at pairs, so that travel in either direction was considered of equal importance. But this network model allows us to view directed influence, from the hub (inner-circle) to the periphery (outer-circle). This is an important dimension, for instance in understanding processes of diffusion across the grammar.

3.5 Summarizing Dialectal Differences

This section has examined national and local dialects using both supervised models (classifiers) and unsupervised models (similarity measures). We began by establishing that there is robust dialectal variation in syntax in written digital registers. Further, both families of models are highly accurate in modeling this variation in a rigorous experimental pipeline. These models agree that population-based variation is concentrated in lower-order concrete constructions and peripheral constructions, and to a lesser degree in more complicated late-stage representations. With the exception of order of emergence, these findings are similar to the location of individual differences. In short, we can view both individual differences and population-based differences as emerging properties created by differences in linguistic experience.

Population-based differences are generally stronger because individuals within the same city have relatively similar linguistic experience and individuals from different cities have very diverging experiences. Importantly, previous work which has relied on arbitrary selections of discrete variables is fundamentally unable to model dialectal variation because there is relatively low agreement between highly abstract core constructions (often chosen as features) and concrete peripheral constructions (rarely if ever chosen as features).

After measuring the magnitude and location of dialectal variation, this section undertook a series of natural experiments to further understand the causes of variation. First, we saw that unsupervised hierarchical clustering methods are able to produce highly accurate taxonomies of national and local dialects.

This tells us about the structure of grammatical variation across the population; in the US, for instance, there is a cluster of southern dialects which spans from east to west but which, interestingly, excludes dialects from the Miami region. We then turned to a regression analysis to understand which factors influence whether two local dialects (at the city-level) are similar or dissimilar. Places with similar linguistic experience have similar grammars. Importantly, though, language contact is more important than population contact as an explanatory factor. This indicates that individual differences, with a similar distribution of variants across the grammar and similar explanatory variables, are more influenced by short-term exposure, while dialectal differences are more influenced by long-term exposure. In other words, dialectal variation seems to result from individual differences which have then spread throughout the population.

These models rely on notions of exposure rather than social concepts like prestige or strong ties. At scale, the population network creates so many exposure situations that variables which are explanatory in small samples lose their explanatory value at a more realistic scale (Laitinen & Fatemi, 2022; Laitinen et al., 2020). Our view, supported by these natural experiments, is that variation is an emergent properties of discovery-device grammars acquired within specific exposure situations. Thus, dialects which have more similar exposure conditions are themselves more similar.

The section ended by viewing the global speech community as a network in which each of 304 cities has some possible exposure to every other city. In this network, each city is a node and syntactic distance is the edge weight that connects nodes. A centrality analysis showed that inner-circle dialects, specifically centered on the UK, are the most central hubs of English. Because this model includes outer-circle dialects, this takes into account which dialects have had the most influence in the formation of World Englishes (Kachru, 1982). This model is useful for exploring asymmetric differences in exposure, where hubs (which have contact with many nonlocal dialects) are less impacted by contact then isolated nodes (which have contact with only a few nonlocal dialects).

Our conclusion is that a great deal of population-based variation can be explained directly by the concept of exposure. Social factors like prestige (or hubs-and-spokes in a network) are important insofar as they influence exposure. From a theoretical perspective, the emergence of grammar and the emergence of grammatical variation can then be explained as the direct and indirect effects of a single complex system. Previous work, with limited sample size in terms of both the population and the grammar, has been unable to view language as a complex system.

4 Variation across Contexts

We have so far considered syntactic variation across individuals and groups of individuals. At the same time, we also know that even the same individuals have very different production across contexts. This fourth section thus shifts to examining variation across register, or the context of production, using a corpus with fifteen distinct written registers. Register variation is hypothesized to be organized around the functions required by particular communicative situations. Thus, we would expect the location of register variation within the grammar to differ from our previous experiments with individual differences and dialectal variation. This section begins by measuring the magnitude and robustness of register variation with a classification-based model and then validating similarity measures for register using a classification task. We then move into a deeper exploration of how the grammar varies across contexts.

4.1 Register as Contextually Defined Exposure

Our basic hypothesis here is that register is a result of contextually defined exposure. In other words, the emergence of grammar depends on linguistic experience and we expect this experience to be organized by communicative situation. Thus, production patterns in one register may differ significantly from production patterns in another. If the grammar is based on a stored linguistic experience – an internal store of representations perhaps structured like an embedding space which compresses and aggregates individual utterances – then this store of representations would also be specific to communicative contexts. If this were the case, then exposure to unique syntactic forms in a context like fiction or legislative speeches would not necessarily translate into production of those forms in other contexts like social media or nonfiction articles.

At the same time, we also expect that register variation is organized around specific functions (Biber, 2012; Biber & Conrad, 2009). This differs from individual and dialectal variation which are not expected to be organized around the functions which a construction is used to fulfill and which thus will be more heterogeneously distributed across constructions. There are many constructions available for expressing any given function, so that function alone is not enough to explain register variation. The hypothesis here is that contextually defined exposure provides an exemplar for which constructions should express a function, so that register results from both (i) the need to express specific functions and (ii) linguistic experience that connects those functions with specific constructions.

This third case-study is important because register variation is rich and pervasive: we cannot study other forms of syntactic variation while ignoring register. The previous sections have largely ignored register in order to focus more precisely on individual or dialectal variation within a single register. Thus, we restricted ourselves to social media data in order to control for the confound of mistaking register variation (which could have similar impacts across many local populations) for dialectal variation (which is unique to each local population). And yet the goal in this Element is to provide a comprehensive theory of syntactic variation at scale. Because there is a tremendous amount of register variation, we must consider its organization within the grammar.

The primary corpora for representing register-specific production are listed in Table 1. These written corpora represent specific contexts of production, from congressional speeches to hotel reviews. The goal is not to catalog an exhaustive set of unique registers in written English but rather to include a sufficient number of example registers to allow generalizations about how register variation is structured in the grammar. There is no exhaustive set of registers: as new contexts come to be, new forms of language use emerge as well (Egbert et al., 2015). These registers all have an inner-circle focus; local dialects could certainly develop their own unique registers but that is not our focus here.

The corpora are divided into seven subregisters. First, formal published texts are represented by books from Project Gutenberg and from the EU Bookshop. Second, formal legislative proceedings are represented by the European Parliament and the US Congress. Third, news articles are represented by both traditional sources (*The New York Times*) and more recent digital-only sources (*Politico* and *Business Insider*). Fourth, informal opinions about fixed topics are represented by hotel reviews and product reviews. Fifth, informal opinions about varied topics are represented by blogs and comments on news articles. Sixth, conversational-style writing is represented by movie subtitles and tweets and TED Talks. Finally, nonfiction articles are represented by Wikipedia and by scientific papers.

A model of register should be able to distinguish between these differing contexts of production. A model which is able to capture register variation by accurately distinguishing between these specific cases will then be able to tell us about the sources of register variation and how it is structured in the grammar. As before, this means that we validate the model using its prediction accuracy before using the model to explore contextual variation in more detail.

The grammar used for modeling individual and dialectal differences was learned entirely from a single register, social media, because that is the only

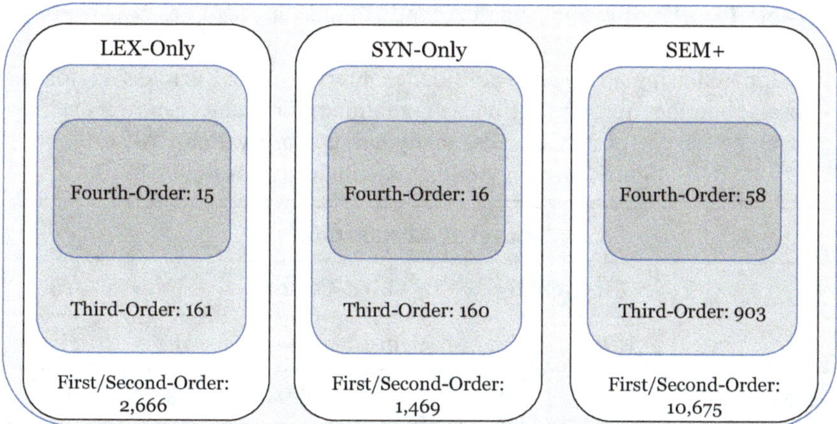

Figure 14 Division of constructions in the grammar by emergence and abstractness for the cross-register grammar.

register used in those previous experiments. Because we are now looking at a range of written registers, we learn a new grammar on an equal mix of corpora drawn from social media, Wikipedia, and general web text. This provides a more generic grammar which, in turn, allows us to better compare these very different written registers. The breakdown of this register-focused grammar is shown in Figure 14, divided by both order of emergence (LEX, SYN, SEM+) as well as by level of abstraction (first/second-order, third-order, fourth-order). The general size is comparable to the grammar shown in Figure 1, with more first-order constructions than more abstract (fourth-order) constructions and more late-stage (SEM+) than early-stage (LEX) constructions. A full inventory of this grammar is available in the supplementary material.

4.2 Magnitude and Robustness: How Much Register Variation?

Our first task is to measure the magnitude and robustness of register variation across the fifteen contexts shown in Table 1. We use a single classifier for all registers but repeat for ten rounds to provide a better estimate of classification performance. Because the overall corpora are quite large in this case, each round has a unique set of samples. We then conduct five-fold cross-validation within each round to provide a total of fifty classifiers (ten rounds of unique data each with five folds). Performance is reported in Table 15 using the f-score to measure accuracy; the minimum and maximum values with a 95% confidence interval are given. As before, the magnitude of variation is shown by the accuracy (higher scores indicate more variation), while robustness over specific samples is shown by the range between minimum and maximum values (a smaller range means more consistent variation).

Table 15 Classification accuracy for distinguishing samples drawn from distinct registers as measured by the f-score. The min and max values are estimated using a Bayesian confidence interval of 95% across five-fold cross-validation. Samples are chosen at random for each of ten rounds, thus averaging the performance across many unique observations. All values are significantly higher than the majority baseline.

	Level of Abstraction					
	First-Order		**Third-Order**		**Fourth-Order**	
	Min	*Max*	*Min*	*Max*	*Min*	*Max*
All Registers	0.97	0.97	0.94	0.94	0.86	0.86
	Order of Emergence					
	LEX		SYN		SEM+	
	Min	*Max*	*Min*	*Max*	*Min*	*Max*
All Registers	0.95	0.95	0.96	0.96	0.96	0.96
	Degree of Centrality					
	Low		**Mid**		**High**	
	Min	*Max*	*Min*	*Max*	*Min*	*Max*
All Registers	0.96	0.96	0.96	0.96	0.94	0.94

The results in Table 15 show that there is even more syntactic variation by context of production than by dialect or individual. For instance, first-order constructions obtain an f-score of 0.97 and late-stage constructions (SEM+) an f-score of 0.96. Register variation is also the most robust: the minimum and maximum estimates of accuracy are the same. Given that register is such a significant source of syntactic variation, it is essential that a theory of syntactic variation include individual differences, dialectal differences, and contextual differences together.

For two of our divisions of the grammar, order of emergence and degree of centrality, there is no major difference in the amount of register variation that is observed. In other words, regardless of whether we focus on core constructions or peripheral construction the f-score is almost exactly the same. The f-score represents classification accuracy which, in turn, represents how well this part of the grammar is able to distinguish between registers. What we see is that all areas of the grammar on these two dimensions are equally subject to variation

Table 16 Average F-Score by Register across level of abstractness. All registers are contained in a single model. The average f-score per register is calculated across ten rounds, each with its own training and testing samples.

Register	First-Order	Third-Order	Fourth-Order
PG Books	1.00	1.00	0.94
EU Bookshop	0.80	0.62	0.57
Wikipedia	1.00	1.00	0.98
Scientific	0.81	0.62	0.52
EU Parliament	1.00	1.00	0.97
US Congress	1.00	1.00	0.96
Print News	1.00	1.00	0.91
Online News	1.00	1.00	0.89
Products	1.00	1.00	0.91
Hotels	1.00	1.00	0.99
Comments	1.00	1.00	0.86
Blogs	1.00	1.00	0.90
Subtitles	1.00	1.00	0.93
TED Talks	0.87	0.58	0.33
TW	1.00	1.00	0.86

across contexts. This is striking because this was not the case for individual and dialectal differences.

The one dimension which does show a difference is level of abstraction: there is a hierarchy from most concrete (0.97) to middle (0.94) to most abstract (0.86). There is less variation in the most abstract constructions. Since this is the only structural difference across the grammar in terms of where register variation is located, we take a closer look at level of abstraction across registers in Table 16. This table shows the f-score for each level of abstraction for each register. The *Support* column indicates the average number of test samples per class for each individual classifier; the results are averaged across multiple iterations as described above. Registers are grouped into pairs, with most groups containing two very similar registers.

Focusing on the most concrete first-order constructions, most registers obtain an f-score of 1.00: perfect prediction accuracy. This means, for instance, that the model has no difficulty distinguishing between blogs and news comments which, in turn, means that there are unique syntactic variants in each that makes such high accuracy possible. Three registers, however, have much lower scores here and throughout the grammar: EU Bookshop, scientific articles, and TED Talks. These three registers are less distinct: they have fewer unique variants which makes reliably identifying them more difficult. Thus, the average in Table 15 disguises the fact that most registers have very high performance.

This differs from dialects, for instance, where classes tend to be more consistent in performance. In part this model depends on the selection of which registers to include, and the selection procedure for registers is more arbitrary than for individuals or dialects. However, the goal is not to provide an exhaustive model of possible registers (an impossible task) but rather to observe a sufficient number of registers to understand how contextual variation differs from population-based variation.

Our conclusion from this section is that register variation is stronger and more robust than individual or dialectal variation. There are simply more syntactic differences between registers. From these classification-based experiments, the only structure to register variation in the grammar is that less abstract constructions tend to have higher variation. However, this conclusion is muddied by the fact that the lower performance is heavily concentrated in just three of the registers. The challenge is that there is simply so much register variation that this experiment has reached its ceiling: we cannot distinguish between categories that reach so high an accuracy. In order to better understand register variation, then, we need to shift to a more difficult task.

4.3 Evaluating Register Similarity Measures

The classification-based experiments in the previous section have shown that register variation is stronger and more robust than both individual differences and dialectal variation. In fact, register variation is so robust that the classifier reached the ceiling in performance: if all parts of the grammar contain sufficient variation to distinguish between registers, then we are no longer able to use this model to explore how this variation is distributed across the grammar. Here we move to similarity measures, as before, to take a second look. These measures are unsupervised, which means that there are no labels provided. Any differences between register therefore emerge naturally from the data rather than being learned from examples. We follow the same methodology as in the previous uses of similarity measures: the distance between two registers is sampled from a population of 1,000 pairs of observations. Cosine distance is calculated over normalized construction frequencies with weights provided by the classifier; the resulting distances are standardized so that we can more easily compare which registers are very similar and which are very different.

We begin by validating these similarity measures using a classification task in Table 17. Here we calculate the average self-similarity for each register and the average similarity to other registers. Any case in which samples from two registers (say, blogs and news comments) are more similar to each other than to themselves is considered a wrong prediction. Thus, the table shows the accuracy in percents: 100% means that all cross-register comparisons are more different than same-register comparisons. For the sake of space, only the first and last category of each dimension is shown (i.e., first-order and fourth-order constructions, but not third-order). The full results are available in the supplementary material. Note that social media data is separated by inner-circle country as an additional test of robustness; we would expect that country has a minimal influence on social media as a register.

These unsupervised measures are remarkably accurate: ranging from 100% (for fourth-order constructions) to 88.8% (for first-order constructions. This means that we can have confidence in general for these measures. We do not need perfect accuracy here; after all, the classification task assumes that all news comments belong to one register and all blogs to another. And yet we could easily imagine instances of blogs that look more like news comments and vice-versa. Thus, we only want an accuracy measure that is high enough to give us confidence in its validity. A further analysis of the validity of similarity measures in this context is available in the supplementary material.[7]

The conclusions from this section are, first, that a similarity-based model of register differences is highly accurate as measured using a classification task. This corresponds with our previous validations and is essential for showing the ground-truth of the model before we start to interpret its representations more closely. Second, the location of register variation within the grammar is more difficult to ascertain because it is present in all areas; thus, classification accuracy with outliers removed makes essentially perfect predictions in all but fourth-order constructions. Relying on similarity measures, then, to locate register variation, we see that core constructions are subject to more variation than peripheral constructions. This is exactly the opposite as individual and This is exactly the opposite of what we see in individual and dialectal differences, our first indication that these phenomena have somewhat different sources.

[7] https://doi.org/10.17605/OSF.IO/A57US.

Table 17 Accuracy of unsupervised similarity measures for categorizing registers. Measure in accuracy (percent correct). The middle category of each dimension is not shown for reasons of space.

	Emergence		Abstraction		Centrality	
	LEX	FULL	*1st*	*4th*	LOW	HIGH
Bookshop	94.1	94.1	94.1	100	94.1	100
Gutenberg	100	100	82.4	100	82.4	100
US Congress	100	100	100	100	100	100
E. Parliament	100	100	100	100	100	100
Digital News	100	100	89.6	100	95.4	100
Print News	100	100	86.5	100	86.5	100
Scientific	89.3	89.3	89.3	100	89.3	100
Wikipedia	100	100	100	100	100	100
Blogs	100	100	85.2	100	85.2	100
Comments	100	100	85.2	100	85.2	100
Hotels	100	100	85.7	100	85.7	100
Products	100	100	85.2	100	85.2	100
Subtitles	100	100	86.4	100	100	100
TED Talks	100	100	100	100	100	88.9
TW (AU)	100	88.0	88.0	100	88.0	100
TW (CA)	100	92.6	85.2	100	85.2	100
TW (IE)	100	100	85.2	100	85.2	100
TW (NZ)	100	96.3	81.5	100	85.2	96.3
TW (UK)	100	95.2	81.0	100	85.7	100
TW (US)	100	100	85.2	100	85.2	100
AVG	*99.2*	*97.8*	*88.8*	*100*	*90.2*	*99.3*

4.4 Exploring Register Differences

Now that we have established the magnitude of register variation and validated both the supervised and unsupervised models, we will use these models to further explore how constructions differ by the context of production. Our first approach is to view the inventory of registers as a network, each connecting to all the others by a similarity value. We can use this distance matrix to understand which registers group together and which are quite different.

To do this we employ hierarchical clustering, as we have done previously for national and local dialects. By creating a taxonomy of registers, we can better understand why some contexts are more similar than others.

Hierarchical clustering takes the estimated syntactic similarity between each register as a single distance matrix and then joins together the most similar registers until a tree is composed that connects all registers. Longer branches in this tree indicate greater differences. The first major distinction in the clusters is between noninteractive contexts (like scientific articles or published books) and interactive contexts (like social media or subtitles or product reviews). In the first case, the author is engaging in a monologue without interruption. In the second case, the author is either directly engaging in a dialogue with other users or, at the very least, responding to and commenting upon early posts (as in, for example, product reviews). Since this is the first major distinction, we provide two clustermaps in Figures 15 and 16, each of which provides further structure within its subgroup.

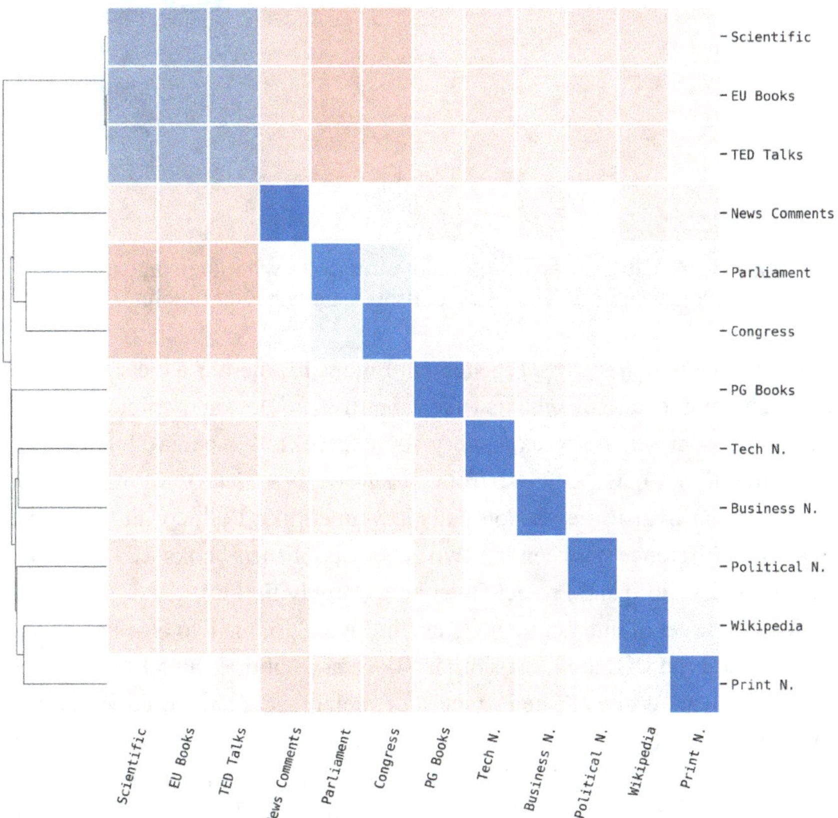

Figure 15 Clustermap of non-interactive registers with late-stage (SEM+) constructions. This is an entirely unsupervised pipeline.

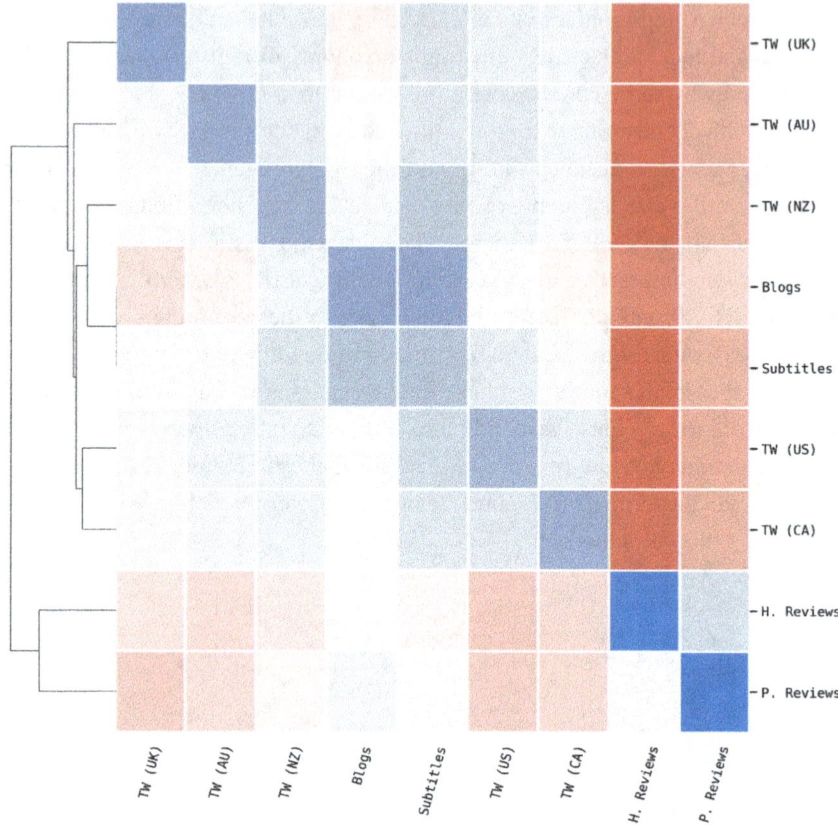

Figure 16 Clustermap of interactive registers with late-stage (SEM+) constructions. This is an entirely unsupervised pipeline.

Within the noninteractive registers, in Figure 15, there is a clear distinction between argumentative contexts (like scientific articles) and opinion contexts (like news comments) and expository contexts (like Wikipedia). Interestingly, more traditional news articles (from *The New York Times*) are more similar to Wikipedia than to newer journalistic venues like Politico. Further, there is a wide difference between the two sets of published books, EU Bookshop (largely nonfiction) and Project Gutenberg (largely fiction).

Within the set of interactive registers, in Figure 16, the two types of reviews (hotels and products) are most similar. Blogs and subtitles also form a closely connected pair. While all the instances of social media are closely connected, they are divided into two groups: North American (US and CA) and Commonwealth (UK, AU, NZ). This shows the impact of dialect; because these labels contain both population-based and context-based information, the clusters do not distinguish between the two source of variation. This is interesting because register is the most defining attribute (which is why all five are closely

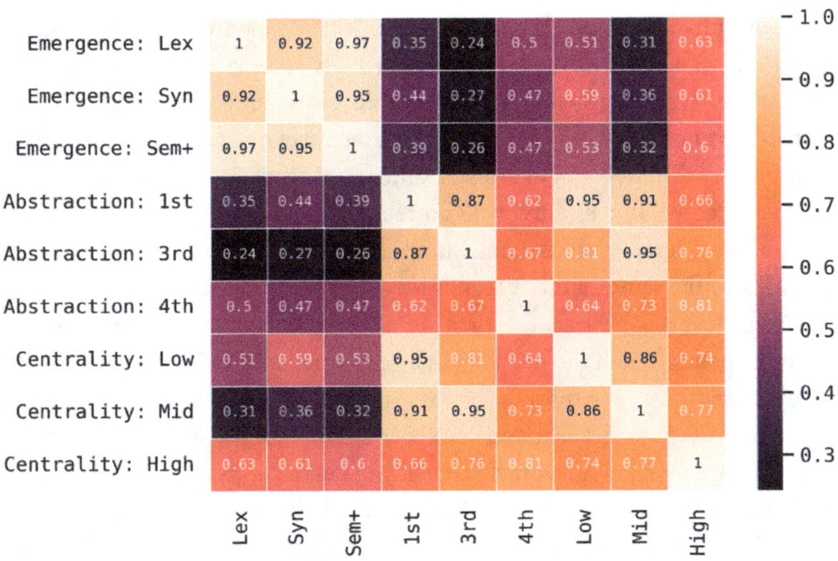

Figure 17 Heatmap of Spearman correlations between ranks of register similarity across subsets of the grammar.

clustered within interactive registers) but geography remains important (which is why there is division by place). It is also possible that distinct populations have developed their own sets of registers; there is no reason to assume that all languages or all dialects would end up with a shared inventory of registers. However, we do not explore this question further here.

This raises the question of how closely related register relationship would be if we looked at different portions of the grammar. For instance, most studies of register focus on a relatively small number of features (although a much higher number than similar work on dialects). How consistent are these register divisions across different nodes of the grammar? This is shown in Figure 17 using Spearman correlations between features. First, we take the pairwise similarity between all combinations of registers. Second, we standardize these across features using the z-score, providing relative ranks of similarity within each portion of the grammar. Finally, we use Spearman correlation to find out if two parts of the grammar reach the same similarities (with a high correlation) or whether we would see very different divisions of registers based on which part of the grammar we happen to be observing (with a low correlation). This is a more precise view of where register is located in the grammar because two models could be accurate in somewhat different ways. For example, the validation of similarity measures in the previous section focused on whether same-register pairs are more similar than cross-register pairs; this ignores the relative ranking of various cross-register pairs.

The results mirror our conclusions from the location of register variation in the grammar. For instance, there is a high correlation across orders of emergence. Thus, register variation is stable across order of emergence, with correlations ranging from 0.92 to 0.97. On the other hand, order of emergence leads to very different sets of register similarities than any part of the grammar based on degree of centrality, with correlations from 0.31 o 0.63. While both parts of the grammar are accurate in grouping together a single register, they do not have the same similarity ranks across different registers.

Within level of abstraction, there is a lower correlation of 0.62 between the most concrete and the most abstract constructions. This increases to 0.87 between first-order and third-order constructions; this mirrors the earlier result that the most abstract constructions differ from other constructions. Level of abstraction is much more closely related with degree of centrality (from 0.64 to 0.95) than to order of emergence (from 0.24 to 0.50). Finally, within degree of centrality, there is a moderate correlation of 0.74 and 0.77 between peripheral (low, mid) and core constructions (high).

These results have two implications: First, because similarity ranks differ by what portion of the grammar we observe, we need to be careful to avoid conclusions about register variation without observing the grammar as a whole. Second, the parts of the grammar in which register variation is most unevenly distributed are level of abstraction and degree of centrality. A defining feature of register variation is that core constructions have more variation than peripheral constructions; this is the opposite of individual and dialectal differences.

Our next question is about the role of function over form in register variation: if contexts differ in the communicative function that needs to be expressed, and if constructions can be distinguished by function, then we would expect register variation to be grouped around specific families of constructions. For instance, we have seen that there is little difference overall between early-stage (Lex) and late-stage (Sem+) portions of the grammar. This is not surprising if register variation is driven by the function of constructions because the order of emergence and the degree of centrality have no impact on what function a construction carries out. In other words, register differences would be concentrated in specific families of constructions but not in a larger portion of the grammar like all abstract or highly schematic constructions.

What we would expect, then, is that register variation is firmly rooted within specific families of constructions, where each family shares a single function. This analysis focuses on third-order constructions; these are not so abstract as fourth-order constructions, which means that there is a more functional consistency within them. A third-order construction is a group of closely related constructions, like different types of phrasal verbs. We would expect, then, that each third-order construction has a relatively consistent function and that some registers will favor one of those functions over others.

For each third-order construction we use mutual information (MI) to measure how much it differs across pairs of registers. More precisely, MI measures the degree to which a feature (construction frequency) is independent from two categorical variables (registers, like Blogs and Wikipedia). If the construction is independent, this means that it is used equally in both registers; this value tends toward 0. On the other hand, if a construction is highly dependent, this means that it is used in one register but not the other; this value tends toward 1. In short, constructions with a low MI do not vary by register and constructions with a high MI do.

The distribution of mutual information across third-order constructions is shown in Figure 18. MI is calculated on pairs of registers, so here we have independent values for each construction showing whether it varies between Wikipedia and TED Talks (two similar registers, on the y-axis) and then whether it varies between Wikipedia and tweets (two very different registers, on the x-axis). Each point is a separate third-order construction. The shape

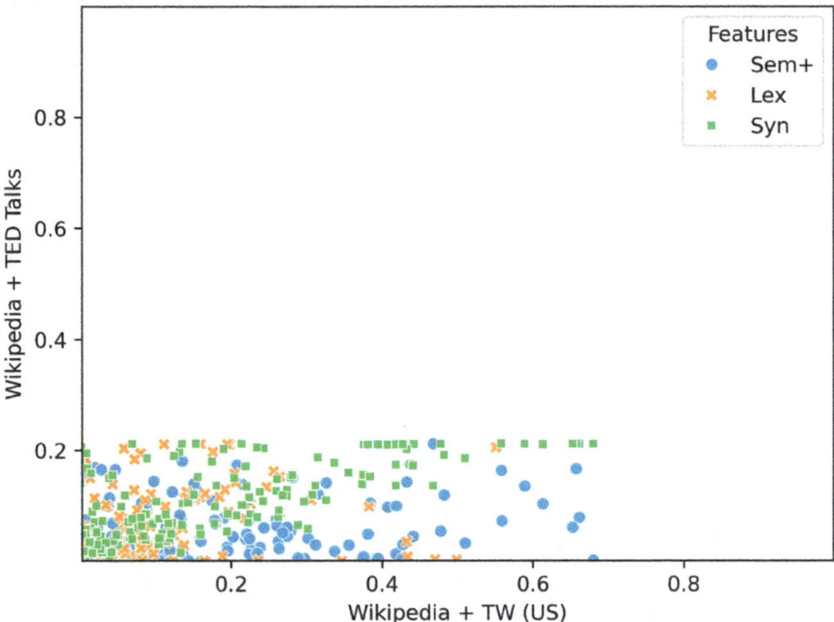

Figure 18 Distribution of variation across third-order constructions as measured by mutual information. Values toward 1 indicate variation and values toward 0 indicate no variation. The y-axis indicates similarity between two similar registers and the x-axis between two very different registers.

and color indicate the order of emergence of each construction. Constructions which have low values in distinguishing between similar registers will be in the bottom portion of the figure, while constructions which have low values for distinguishing between very different registers will be in the left portion of the figure.

Essentially, this figure shows three things: First, that many constructions (especially earlier stage constructions) are not different by register. The highest concentration of points is in the bottom left, with MI below 0.2 for both comparisons. Second, the two similar registers (y-axis) have no highly variant constructions: the same functions are prevalent in both. And, third, a significant number of third-order constructions differ across the more distantly-related registers (x-axis). This figure gives a finer view of register variation across constructions: the reason that order of emergence has no impact on model performance is that there is strong variation in at least some families of constructions regardless of the types of representation they contain.

We can contrast this with the comparison within interactive written registers in Figure 19, with a comparison of blogs with US tweets (y-axis) and with subtitles (x-axis). First, we see that mutual information is quite low throughout;

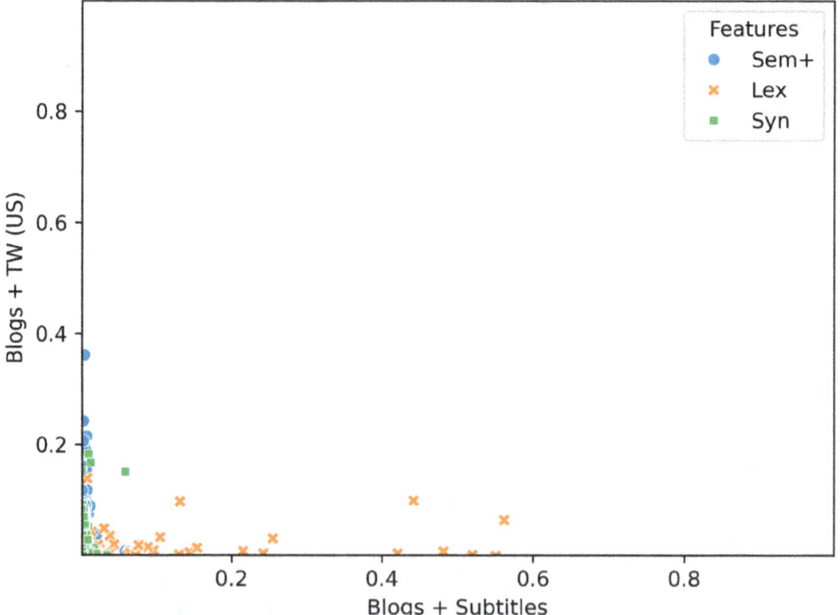

Figure 19 Distribution of variation across third-order constructions as measured by mutual information. Values toward 1 indicate variation and values toward 0 indicate no variation. Both the y-axis and the x-axis reflect similar registers.

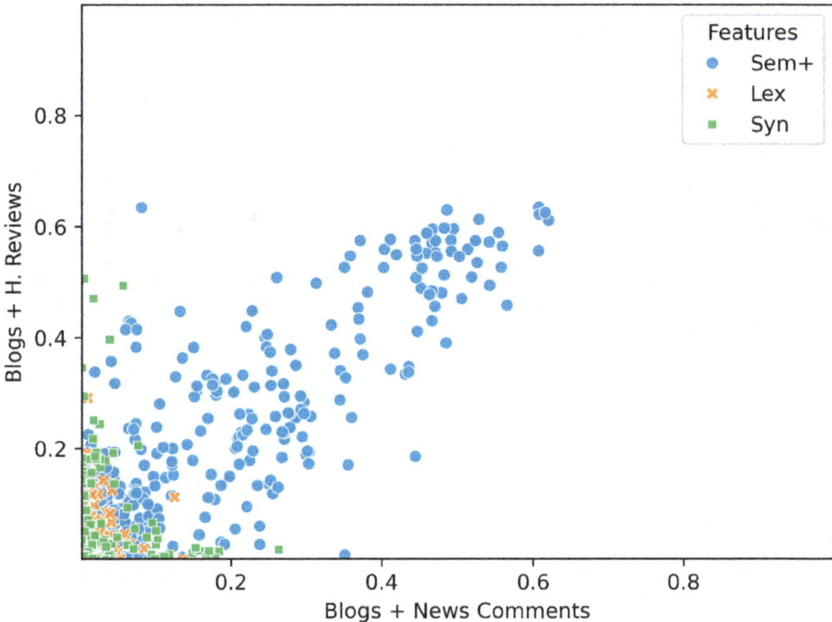

Figure 20 Distribution of variation across third-order constructions as measured by mutual information. Values toward 1 indicate variation and values toward 0 indicate no variation. Both the y-axis and the x-axis reflect different registers.

the same number of third-order constructions are plotted but most are too insignificant to appear. Interestingly, some early-stage lexical constructions differ with subtitles while only a few late-state SEM+ constructions differ with tweets. Otherwise, there is functional consistency across these registers.

A third pattern is shown in Figure 20, showing two sets of equi-distant pairs: blogs and hotel reviews (y-axis) together with blogs and news comments (x-axis). This figure shows an interesting trend in which almost all earlier-stage constructions are concentrated in the bottom left; this means that these constructions have no variation across these registers. Within late-stage constructions, though, most third-order constructions follow the diagonal; this means that they are subject to roughly the same amount of variation between each pair. The reason they are subject to same amount of variation is that the functional difference between the two comparisons is quite similar.

The point of these figures has been to look at register variation within families of constructions. If register variation is structured around the functions which a construction expresses, and if functions are shared within most third-order constructions, then we would expect that registers which share similar contexts (such as interactive written registers) will have few differences at the

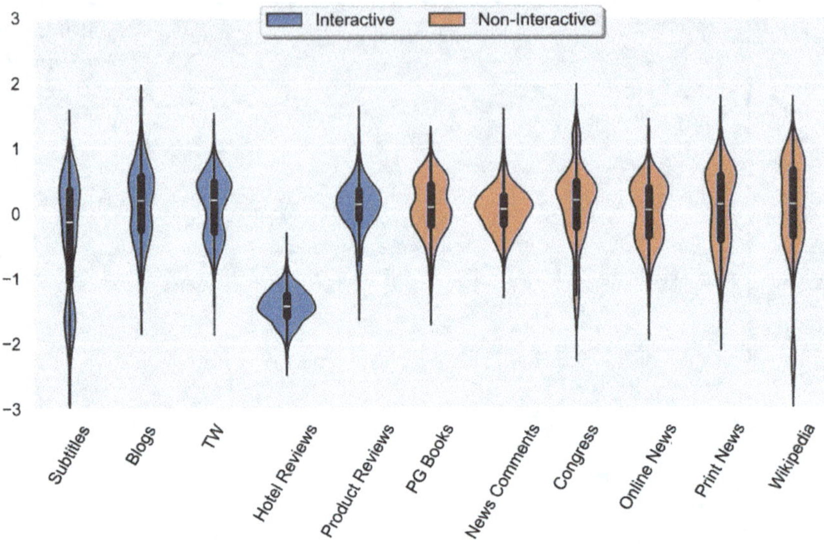

Figure 21 Homogeneity by Register with Late-Stage SEM+ Constructions.

third-order level. This is precisely what we see: register variation is organized around groups with shared functions and, within similar registers, the mutual information tends to be low, indicating less variation by construction.

Much of the analysis of register variation up to this point has focused on the estimated mean similarity within and between contexts of production. Here we look at homogeneity by using violin plots to visualize the distribution of 1,000 pairs of samples from each register. These are located within a standardized space. This is shown in Figure 21, where higher values indicate high distance between samples from the same register and lower values indicate lower distance; lower thus means more similar.

We see in Figure 21 that some registers are more heterogeneous, both in terms of the overall range of similarity and in the consistency of its distribution. Hotel reviews, for instance, are quite homogeneous while subtitles are rather heterogeneous. If differences between registers are driven by functions needed within specific communicative contexts, this implies that some registers have a more heterogeneous context. For instance, hotel reviews have a very narrow rhetorical purpose of describing the quality of a hotel stay, but subtitles include closed captions for many types of films and Project Gutenberg books encompass many genres both fiction and nonfiction. This figure thus estimates the degree to which each source has a narrowly constrained context.

Our final experiment in this section focuses on understanding the distinction between register variation (across contexts) and dialectal variation (across populations). In particular, our goal is to understand how each type of variation

Table 18 Classification accuracy for distinguishing country-level tweets from either (i) comparable tweets from other countries or (ii) samples from other registers. Performance is estimated with a 95% confidence interval using each national dialect (AU, CA, IE, NZ, UK, US) as the pivot which is included in both models.

	Level of Abstraction					
	First-Order		**Third-Order**		**Fourth-Order**	
	Min	*Max*	*Min*	*Max*	*Min*	*Max*
Dialect	0.99	0.99	0.77	0.78	0.39	0.39
Register	1.00	1.00	1.00	1.00	0.95	0.96
	Order of Emergence					
	LEX		SYN		SEM+	
	Min	*Max*	*Min*	*Max*	*Min*	*Max*
Dialect	0.92	0.92	0.85	0.86	0.98	0.99
Register	1.00	1.00	1.00	1.00	1.00	1.00
	Degree of Centrality					
	Low		**Mid**		**High**	
	Min	*Max*	*Min*	*Max*	*Min*	*Max*
Dialect	0.99	0.99	0.87	0.87	0.65	0.66
Register	1.00	1.00	1.00	1.00	1.00	1.00

is distributed across the entire grammar; previous work, with access only to limited discrete features, has not been able to address this question. Our basic approach is to use country-level tweets as a pivot: in one classifier we train a model to distinguish between a single register (tweets) across six national dialects (US, UK, CA, AU, NZ, IE). Then, in another classifier, we train a model to distinguish between a single dialect of tweets with five other registers (blogs, news comments, news articles, novels, and Wikipedia). The first model is focused on distinguishing between dialects and the second on distinguishing between registers, but both share one subcorpus (i.e., tweets from the US). This design is then repeated across parts of the grammar and with each national dialect serving as the pivot.

Our analysis starts with the magnitude and robustness of each type of variation, as represented by the f-score and the robustness of the f-score across specific rounds with unique test sets. This is shown in Table 18. These results replicate our earlier findings about magnitude and robustness under a slightly different setting: these models are based on the generic-register grammar and dialect samples are aggregated by country rather than by city. The patterns remain the same, however: register variation is stronger and more consistent, with perfect accuracy in all parts of the grammar except for the most abstract fourth-order constructions. Dialectal variation is concentrated in more concrete parts of the grammar (with performance declining steeply with more abstract constructions) and in peripheral parts of the grammar (with performance declining significantly with more central constructions). These results mirror what we have seen previously: first, if registers differ in the functions that need to be expressed, then even highly abstract constructions will differ; second, if dialectal variation is a result of differing linguistic experience (and if immediate linguistic experience consists of more concrete constructions which are then generalized into more abstract families), then dialectal variation will be weak in the abstract and core parts of the grammar. The high accuracy of both tasks allows us to proceed with the comparison of register and dialect using feature weights derived from these models.

Our main analysis is focused on the feature weights for each construction in a given portion of the grammar. The model used here, a Linear SVM, applies a weighting to each construction as part of the prediction process. These weights are centered on zero, so that larger absolute values indicate that a construction is more predictive of a given class and thus more unique to that class. Positive values mean that a construction is more likely in a class and negative values mean that a construction is less likely in a class. In our set-up, the same data from each dialect is compared first with other national dialects in the same register and second with other registers. Thus, we can compare the feature weights extracted from these two models to compare how register vs dialectal variation is distributed across the grammar.

The results are shown at a high level using the heatmap of Pearson correlations in Figure 22. Each row is a specific part of the grammar and each column is a dialect used as a pivot to compare register and dialect in that portion of the grammar. A high correlation would mean that the same constructions are useful for distinguishing the same samples for both register and dialect; a low correlation means that the classification of register and dialect depends on different parts of the grammar. This heatmap shows that correlation is low, especially in those parts of the grammar (like first-order constructions) which are most accurate for the dialect prediction task. This means, in order words, that variation in register and dialect is not located in the same constructions.

The distribution of feature weights is visualized in more detail in Figure 23 which shows the absolute value (both positive and negative evidence) for each

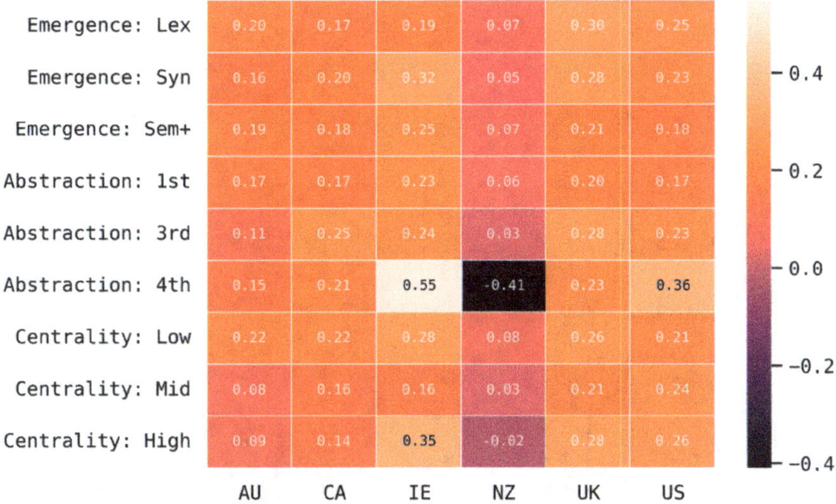

Figure 22 Heatmap showing Pearson correlations between feature weights for samples of tweets representing national dialects across two Linear SVM models: the first distinguishes the dialect from other national dialects and the second distinguishes the social media register from other registers. High correlation means that the same constructions are in variation by register and dialect.

first-order construction. Predictive power for the dialect model is shown on the y-axis and for the register model on the x-axis. Higher values indicate that a construction is more unique to a given dialect. We take the sum of feature weights for each class in the model and then take the average of this across models to represent the non-dialect-specific weighting of constructions. This is a KDE plot of the distribution, so that that inner ring shows the core part of the distribution and the outer rings the tail of the distribution.

If the same constructions were subject to variation across both registers and dialects, then we would see many constructions on the diagonal line. This is not the case. Instead, constructions tend to have predictive power on one axis. What we see here is that register variation is characterized by a smaller number of very predictive constructions (at the first-order level), so that the average predictive power is low. Dialectal variation, on the other hand, is characterized by a relatively small amount of predictive power across many constructions.

This is compatible with the idea that population-based variation is based mainly on differences in linguistic experience (exposure), because first-order constructions serve as the starting point for generalizing to more abstract constructions. In other words, register variation is structured around functions, so that there is a great deal of variation but it is concentrated within specific constructions (which do not appear on this plot because they are low in number).

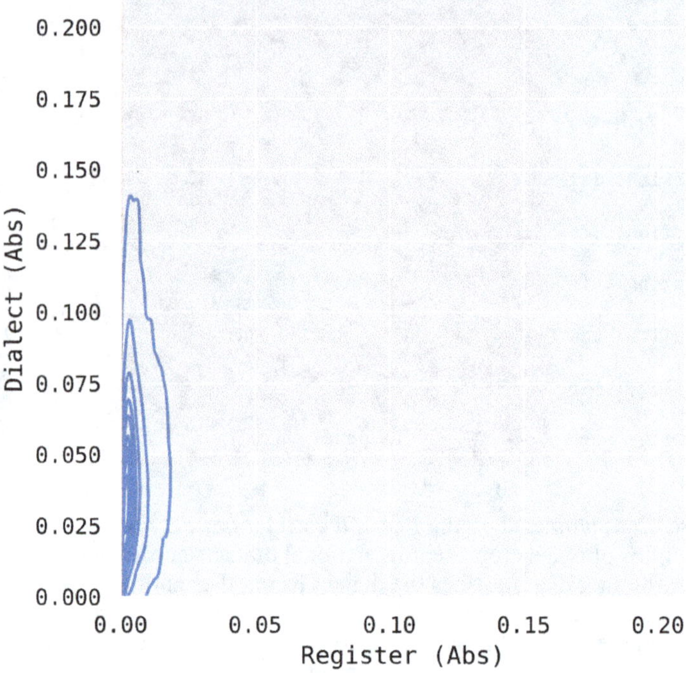

Figure 23 KDE distribution plot showing cumulative feature weights for classifying dialects (y-axis) and registers (x-axis) with first-order constructions. Feature weights are summed across classes to emphasize those constructions which are predictive of any class; the absolute values are shown, merging both positive and negative evidence.

Population-based variation, however, is structured around differences that arise from differences in linguistic experience; these differences are not based on function and as a result are distributed across many constructions. Dialectal variation is greatly reduced as constructions are generalized into more schematic representations which cover many distinct lower-level constructions. But register variation remains strong even in abstract constructions because abstract constructions still differ in function.

4.5 Summarizing Register Differences

This section has shown that register variation is even more robust in the grammar than individual differences and dialectal differences. Both supervised models (classifiers) and unsupervised models (similarity measures) are highly accurate, providing another validated case-study of syntactic variation. The analysis in this section has shown some fundamental differences between types of variation, however, beginning with where it is located in the grammar. Individual differences are concentrated in less abstract constructions and, to a lesser degree, within peripheral construction. But there are no individual differences across order of emergence (c.f., Table 5). Similarly, population-based differences are concentrated in less abstract and peripheral constructions, with a smaller concentration in late-stage constructions (c.f., Table 9). Differences across registers, however, are instead distributed rather evenly across the grammar, with high performance in all areas (c.f., Table 15). The strongest single division in the grammar, shown with similarity measures (c.f., the supplementary material), is that there is greater variation in core constructions. Thus, register differences are quite different from individual and dialectal differences.

Why? This section has taken a number of approaches to understand what causes these different patterns, focusing on the idea that register variation (but not individual differences or dialectal differences) is organized specifically around the function rather than the form of constructions. First, we saw that using hierarchical clustering to build a tree of registers makes a major distinction between interactive registers (like social media) and noninteractive registers (like Wikipedia). By implication, the difference between interactive and noninteractive contexts is the set of functions which need to be expressed. Second, we saw that registers with a focused rhetorical purpose (like hotel reviews) are much more homogeneous than those without a focused purpose. Third, we saw that using mutual information as a measure of the relationship between individual constructions and registers shows that some third-order constructions are sharply different between similar comparisons (interactive-to-interactive) and nonsimilar comparisons (interactive-to-noninteractive). These figures also showed that properties like the order of emergence are irrelevant to the organization of register variation. Finally, we used geo-located social media data as a pivot to compare classifiers trained to distinguish between registers from those trained to distinguish between dialects. Constructions which vary on one dimension do not vary on the other dimension. In all these attributes, contextual variation is unique. Although this section has worked with individual constructional features, the supplementary material contains a further exploration that uses dimension reduction to first create feature bundles.[8]

These results are all compatible with the idea that registers emphasize certain functions and thus select constructions based on the functions which they express. This is why register variation is not impacted by order of emergence or level of abstraction: what matters is the function and highly schematic constructions can still differ in function. In fact, some of the strongest features are core constructions because these are frequently observed but still function-specific.

[8] https://doi.org/10.17605/OSF.IO/A57US.

This does not mean that register variation is unrelated to exposure. For instance, we have seen that the social media register by country is split between commonwealth variants and North American variants. Thus, the connection between functions and registers is not invariant. Why? Grammars are highly redundant, with many syntactic tools available for expressing any given function: we might have a score of constructions which can carry out a given register-specific function. The preference for a subset of those constructions is still a result of exposure to previous production within that register. If this is the case, then we would expect that languages and dialects could have very different sets of registers. For instance, the novel might be a common register, but this does not mean that American novels and Turkish novels and Chinese novels all have the same set of subregisters. This is precisely what we see with social media, with different variants within specific populations. There is, unfortunately, an inner-circle bias within our register-specific corpora. We hypothesize that including more outer-circle registers would allow us to see more variation in the connection between function and register, conditioned by exposure.

5 Conclusions

This Element has taken a comprehensive approach to modeling syntactic variation at scale. We have seen that the grammar is a complex network, for instance with dialectal differences being concentrated in concrete and peripheral constructions, while register differences are concentrated in core constructions. And we have seen that the population is also a complex network, with factors like the amount of contact with nonlocal populations providing significant predictive power about whether two local dialects will be more similar.

The essential finding from this work is that variation is an emergent property of a complex network (the grammar) used across another complex network (the population). Methods which try to understand this emergent property using unrepresentative samples are fundamentally flawed. By analogy, this is like trying to understand global changes in climate patterns given only observations from Reno, Nevada. For example, we have seen that individual differences and dialectal differences and register differences all vary significantly depending on which portion of the grammar we observe. And yet most work relies on small, arbitrary selections of features. Unfortunately, one attribute of a complex system is that a property of a part is not a property of the whole.

This Element has viewed syntactic variation across three settings: individual differences among speakers in 93 cities across two countries, dialectal differences among 304 local dialects across 14 countries, and contextual differences across 15 written registers. These three sources of variation each provide an important view on why and how the grammar comes to vary. Previous work, however, has almost uniformly focused on one type of variation. By comparing all three types of variation, this Element has been able to show, for instance, that variants are concentrated in unique parts of the grammar: order of emergence has no impact on individual differences, dialectal variation is much reduced in highly abstract and core constructions, and register variation is organized around function more than form and is strongest in core constructions. Mapping the location of syntactic variation in this way is only possible if we use the same set of methods to model all three branches of variation together.

The story of syntactic variation as an emergent property of language is relatively simple: individuals within a single population all have slightly different sets of linguistic experience. Further, those places which have more population contact and more language contact have more unique experiences. At the same time, the discovery-device grammar begins by forming relatively concrete first-order constructions directly from exposure. Thus, groups with different sets of exposure end up with very different sets of first-order constructions.

But during the emergence of the grammar, the discovery-device increasingly generalizes to higher-order representations. Thus, differences in exposure have less direct impact within higher-order constructions. The generalization mechanism is shared across speakers. As a result, it serves to smooth away differences in first-order constructions. This is why individual differences and dialectal differences are weak in fourth-order constructions and core constructions, both the result of such generalization processes.

Individual and dialectal differences are based on different sets of exposure but having nothing at all to do with the functions which a construction is used to express. For this reason, variation along these dimensions is distributed equally across functions. Register differences, however, result from specific contexts requiring specific functions. The relationship between context and function is not fixed: in social media, for instance, there is a divide between North American mappings and Commonwealth mappings, where a *mapping* is a preference for certain constructions given a need for certain functions. Thus, register is organized around function and is equally robust across level of abstraction and order of emergence and degree of centrality but still depends on exposure for establishing which constructions are connected with which registers.

To conclude: language is a complex system. Syntactic variation is an emergent property of that system which can only be understood properly at scale because each part of the system is a result of processes which are operating upon the whole. This Element has used corpus-based computational models to examine this complex system. The result is a series of highly accurate models which show that syntactic variation is remarkably robust even in written contexts. Not only is variation itself robust but it is also relatively simple to explain once we have focused our view on the complex system as a whole. By enabling us to observe variation in the system itself, computational methods have fundamentally altered our understanding of how and why grammars are continuously changing.

References

Alishahi, A., & Stevenson, S. (2008). A computational model of early argument structure acquisition. *Cognitive Science*, *32*(5), 789–834.

Bamman, D., Eisenstein, J., & Schnoebelen, T. (2014). Gender identity and lexical variation in social media. *Journal of Sociolinguistics*, *18*(2), 135–160.

Barak, L., & Goldberg, A. (2017). Modeling the partial productivity of constructions. In *Proceedings of the 2017 spring symposium on computational construction grammar and natural language understanding* (pp. 131–138). Association for the Advancement of Artificial Intelligence.

Beckner, C., Ellis, N., Blythe, R., et al. (2009). Language is a complex adaptive system: position paper. *Language Learning*, *59*, 1–26.

Beuls, K., & Van Eecke, P. (2023). Fluid construction grammar: State of the art and future outlook. In *Proceedings of the first international workshop on construction grammars and NLP* (pp. 41–50). Association for Computational Linguistics.

Biber, D. (2012). Register as a predictor of linguistic variation. *Corpus Linguistics and Linguistic Theory*, *8*(1), 9–37.

Biber, D., & Conrad, S. (2009). *Register, genre, and style*. Cambridge University Press.

Biber, D., Egbert, J., & Keller, D. (2020). Reconceptualizing register in a continuous situational space. *Corpus Linguistics and Linguistic Theory*, *16*(3), 581–616.

Campello, R., Moulavi, D., & Sander, J. (2013). Advances in knowledge discovery and data mining. PAKDD 2013. In J. Pei, V. S. Tseng, L. Cao, H. Motoda, & G. Xu (Eds.), (Vol. 7819, pp. 160–172). Springer.

Campello, R., Moulavi, D., Zimek, A., & Sandler, J. (2015). Hierarchical density estimates for data clustering, visualization, and outlier detection. *ACM Transactions on Knowledge Discovery from Data*, *10*(1), pp. 1–51.

Collins, P. (2012). Singular agreement in there existentials: An intervarietal corpus-based study. *English World-Wide*, *33*(1), 53–68.

Cook, P., & Brinton, J. (2017). Building and evaluating web corpora representing national varieties of English. *Language Resources and Evaluation*, *51*(3), 643–662.

Croft, W. (2013). Radical construction grammar. In T. Hoffmann & G. Trousdale (Eds.), *The Oxford handbook of construction grammar* (pp. 211–232). Oxford University Press.

Davies, M., & Fuchs, R. (2015). Expanding horizons in the study of World Englishes with the 1.9 billion word Global Web-based English Corpus (GloWbE). *English World-Wide*, *36*(1), 1–28.

Diessel, H. (2023). *The constructicon: Taxonomies and networks*. Cambridge University Press.

Donoso, G., Sánchez, D., & Sanchez, D. (2017). Dialectometric analysis of language variation in Twitter. In *Proceedings of the workshop on NLP for similar languages, varieties and dialects* (pp. 16–25). Association for Computational Linguistics.

Doumen, J., Beuls, K., & Van Eecke, P. (2023). Modelling language acquisition through syntactico-semantic pattern finding. In A. Vlachos & I. Augenstein (Eds.), *Findings of the association for computational linguistics: Eacl 2023* (pp. 1347–1357). Association for Computational Linguistics.

Dunn, J. (2017). Computational learning of construction grammars. *Language & Cognition*, *9*(2), 254–292.

Dunn, J. (2018a). Finding variants for construction-based dialectometry: A corpus-based approach to regional cxgs. *Cognitive Linguistics*, *29*(2), 275–311.

Dunn, J. (2018b). Modeling the complexity and descriptive adequacy of construction grammars. *In proceedings of the society for computation in linguistics* (pp. 81–90), Association for Computational Linguistics.

Dunn, J. (2018c). Multi-unit directional measures of association moving beyond Pairs of words. *International Journal of Corpus Linguistics*, *23*(2), 183–215.

Dunn, J. (2019a). Frequency vs. Association for constraint selection in usage-based construction grammar. In *Proceedings of the workshop on cognitive modeling and computational linguistics* (p. 117–128). Association for Computational Linguistics.

Dunn, J. (2019b). Global syntactic variation in seven languages: Toward a computational dialectology. *Frontiers in Artificial Intelligence*, *2*, 15.

Dunn, J. (2020). Mapping languages: The corpus of global language use. *Language Resources and Evaluation*, *54*, 999–1018.

Dunn, J. (2022). Exposure and emergence in usage-based grammar: Computational experiments in 35 languages. *Cognitive Linguistics*, *33*, 659–699.

Dunn, J. (2023a). Exploring the constructicon: Linguistic analysis of a computational CxG. In *Proceedings of the first international workshop on construction grammars and nlp* (pp. 1–11). Association for Computational Linguistics.

Dunn, J. (2023b). Syntactic variation across the grammar: Modelling a complex adaptive system. *Frontiers in Complex Systems, Volume 1.*

Dunn, J. (2024). *Computational construction grammar: A usage-based approach*. Cambridge University Press.

Dunn, J., Coupe, T., & Adams, B. (2020). Measuring linguistic diversity during COVID-19. In *Proceedings of the fourth workshop on natural language processing and computational social science* (pp. 1–10). Association for Computational Linguistics.

Dunn, J., & Nijhof, W. (2022). Language identification for austronesian languages. In *Proceedings of the 13th international conference on language resources and evaluation* (pp. 6530–6539). European Language Resources Association.

Dunn, J., & Nini, A. (2021). Production vs perception: The role of individuality in usage-based grammar induction. In *Proceedings of the workshop on cognitive modeling and computational linguistics* (pp. 149–159). Association for Computational Linguistics.

Dunn, J., & Tayyar Madabushi, H. (2021). Learned construction grammars converge across registers given increased exposure. In *Conference on computational natural language learning* (pp. 268–278). Association for Computational Linguistics.

Dąbrowska, E. (2021). How writing changes languages. In *Language change: The impact of english as a lingua franca* (pp. 75–94). Cambridge University Press.

Egbert, J., Biber, D., & Davies, M. (2015). Developing a bottom-up, user-based method of web register classification. *Journal of the Association for Information Science and Technology*, *66*(9), 1817–1831.

Eisenstein, J., O'Connor, B., Smith, N., & Xing, E. (2014). Diffusion of lexical change in social media. *PloSOne*, *10*, 1371.

Fagyal, Z., Swarup, S., Escobar, A. M., Gasser, L., & Lakkaraju, K. (2010). Centers and peripheries: Network roles in language change. *Lingua*, *120*(8), 2061–2079.

Gentzkow, M., Shapiro, J., & Taddy, M. (2018). *Congressional record for the 43rd–114th congresses: Parsed speeches and phrase counts* (Tech. Rep.). Stanford Libraries.

Goldberg, A. (2006). *Constructions at work: The nature of generalization in language*. Oxford University Press.

Goldsmith, J. (2015). Towards a new empiricism for linguistics. In N. Chater, A. Clark, J. Goldsmith, & A. Perfors (Eds.), *Empiricism and language learnability* (pp. 58–105). Oxford University Press.

Gonçalves, B., Loureiro-Porto, L., Ramasco, J. J., & Sánchez, D. (2018). Mapping the americanization of english in space and time. *PLOS ONE*, *13*(5), 1–15.

Gonçalves, B., & Sánchez, D. (2014). Crowdsourcing dialect characterization through twitter. *PLOS ONE*, *9*(11), 1–6.

Grafmiller, J., & Szmrecsanyi, B. (2018). Mapping out particle placement in Englishes around the world A study in comparative sociolinguistic analysis. *Language Variation and Change*, *30*(3), 385–412.

Greenbaum, S. (1996). *Comparing english worldwide: The international corpus of English*. Clarendon Press.

Grieve, J. (2011). A regional analysis of contraction rate in written Standard American English. *International Journal of Corpus Linguistics*, *16*(4), 514–546.

Grieve, J. (2012). A statistical analysis of regional variation in adverb position in a corpus of written Standard American English. *Corpus Linguistics and Linguistic Theory*, *8*(1), 39–72.

Grieve, J. (2016). *Regional variation in written American English*. Cambridge University Press.

Grieve, J., Montgomery, C., Nini, A., Murakami, A., & Guo, D. (2019). Mapping lexical dialect variation in British English using Twitter. *Frontiers in Artificial Intelligence*, *2*, 11.

Grünwald, P. (2007). *The minimum description length principle*. MIT Press.

Hollmann, W., & Siewierska, A. (2011). The status of frequency, schemas, and identity in cognitive sociolinguistics A case study on definite article reduction. *Cognitive Linguistics*, *22*(1), 25–54.

Huang, Z., Wu, X., Jarcia, A., Fik, T., & Tatem, A. (2013). An open-access modeled passenger flow matrix for the global air network in 2010. *PlosONE*, *8*(5), e64317.

Kachru, B. E. (1982). *The Other tongue: English across cultures*. University of Illinois Press.

Kesarwani, A. (2018). *New york times comments*. Kaggle.

Kidd, E., & Donnelly, S. (2020). Individual differences in first language acquisition. *Annual Review of Linguistics*, *6*, 319–340.

Laitinen, M., & Fatemi, M. (2022). Big and rich social networks in computational sociolinguistics. In P. Rautionaho, H. Parviainen, M. Kaunisto, & A. Nurmi (Eds.), *Social and regional variation in world Englishes: Local and global perspectives* (pp. 1–25). Routledge.

Laitinen, M., Fatemi, M., & Lundberg, J. (2020). Size matters: Digital social networks and language change. *Frontiers in Artificial Intelligence*, *3*.

Langacker, R. (1987). *Foundations of cognitive grammar*. Stanford University Press.

Leclercq, B., & Morin, C. (2023). No equivalence: A new principle of no synonymy. *Constructions*, *15*.

Li, J. (2012). *Hotel reviews dataset* (Tech. Rep.). Carnegie Mellon University.

Lison, P., & Tiedemann, J. (2016). OpenSubtitles2016: Extracting large parallel corpora from movie and TV subtitles. In *Proceedings of the international conference on language resources and evaluation* (pp. 923–929). European Language Resources Association.

Lucy, L., & Bamman, D. (2021). Characterizing english variation across social media communities with bert. *Transactions of the Association for Computational Linguistics*, *9*, 538–556.

McKenzie, G., & Adams, B. (2018). A data-driven approach to exploring similarities of tourist attractions through online reviews. *Journal of Location Based Services*, *12*(2), 94–118.

Mocanu, D., Baronchelli, A., Perra, N., et al. (2013). The Twitter of babel: Mapping world languages through microblogging platforms. *PLOSOne*, *10*, 1371.

Nevens, J., Doumen, J., Van Eecke, P., & Beuls, K. (2022). Language acquisition through intention reading and pattern finding. In *Proceedings of the 29th international conference on computational linguistics* (pp. 15–25). International Committee on Computational Linguistics.

Nini, A. (2023). *A theory of linguistic individuality for authorship analysis*. Cambridge University Press.

Ortman, M. (2018). *Wikipedia sentences*. Kaggle.

Parsons, A. (2019). *NY Times Article Lead Paragraphs 1851–2017* (Tech. Rep.). Kaggle.

Perek, F., & Patten, A. L. (2019). Towards an English constructicon using patterns and frames. *International Journal of Corpus Linguistics*, *24*(3), 354–384.

Rae, J. W., Potapenko, A., Jayakumar, S. M., & Lillicrap, T. P. (2020). Compressive transformers for long-range sequence modelling. In *International conference on learning representations* (pp. 1–9). ICRL.

Reimers, N., & Gurevych, I. (2020). Making monolingual sentence embeddings multilingual using knowledge distillation. In *Proceedings of the conference on empirical methods in natural language processing* (pp. 4512–4525). Association for Computational Linguistics.

Schler, J., Koppel, M., Argamon, S., & Pennebaker, J. (2006). Effects of age and gender on blogging. In *Proceedings of aaai spring symposium on computational approaches for analyzing weblogs.* Association for the Advancement of Artificial Intelligence (pp. 1–7).

Schneider, E. W. (2020). Calling englishes as complex dynamic systems: Diffusion and restructuring. In A. Mauranen & S. Vetchinnikova (Eds.), *Language change: The impact of english as a lingua franca* (pp. 15–43). Cambridge University Press.

Soares, F., Moreira, V., & Becker, K. (2018). A large parallel corpus of full-text scientific articles. In *Proceedings of the international conference on language resources and evaluation.* European Language Resource Association.

Szmrecsanyi, B. (2013). *Grammatical variation in British English dialects: A study in corpus-based dialectometry*. Cambridge University Press.

Szmrecsanyi, B., & Grafmiller, J. (2023). *Comparative variation analysis: Grammatical alternations in world englishes*. Cambridge University Press.

Szmrecsanyi, B., Grafmiller, J., Heller, B., & Rothlisberger, M. (2016). Around the world in three alternations Modeling syntactic variation in varieties of English. *English World-Wide*, *37*(2), 109–137.

Szmrecsanyi, B., Grafmiller, J., & Rosseel, L. (2019). Variation-based distance and similarity modeling: A case study in world Englishes. *Frontiers in Artificial Intelligence*, *2*, 23.

Tiedemann, J. (2012). Parallel data, tools and interfaces in OPUS. In *Proceedings of the international conference on language resources and evaluation* (pp. 2214–2218). European Language Resources Association.

Trudgill, P. (2014). Diffusion, drift, and the irrelevance of media influence. *Journal of Sociolinguistics*, *18*(2), 213–222.

Wible, D., & Tsao, N. (2010). StringNet as a computational resource for discovering and investigating linguistic constructions. In *Proceedings of the workshop on extracting and using constructions in computational linguistics* (pp. 25–31). Association for Computational Linguistics.

Wible, D., & Tsao, N. (2020). Constructions and the problem of discovery: A case for the paradigmatic: *Corpus Linguistics and Linguistic Theory*, *16*(1), 67–93.

Wieling, M., Nerbonne, J., & Baayen, R. H. (2011). Quantitative social dialectology: Explaining linguistic variation geographically and socially. *PloS One*, *6*, 9.

Zhang, X., Zhao, J., & LeCun, Y. (2015). Character-level convolutional networks for text classification. In *Proceedings of the international conference on neural information processing systems* (pp. 649–657). Neural Information Processing Systems Foundation.

Acknowledgments

This work has benefited greatly from previous and ongoing collaborations with Andrea Nini, Ben Adams, Sidney Wong, Harish Tayyar Madabushi, Steven Coats, Cameron Morin, and Shlomo Argamon.

Cambridge Elements

Construction Grammar

About the Series

Construction Grammar is the leading cognitive theory of syntax. The present Elements series will survey its theoretical building blocks, show how Construction Grammar can capture various linguistic phenomena across a wide range of typologically different languages, and identify emerging frontier topics from a theoretical, empirical and applied perspective.

Cambridge Elements ☰

Construction Grammar

Elements in the Series

The Constructicon: Taxonomies and Networks
Holger Diessel

Constructionist Approaches: Past, Present, Future
Tobias Ungerer and Stefan Hartmann

Copilots for Linguists: AI, Constructions, and Frames
Tiago Timponi Torrent, Thomas Hoffmann, Arthur Lorenzi Almeida and Mark Turner

Can Construction Grammar Be Proven Wrong?
Bert Cappelle

Constructions and Compositionality: Cognitive and Computational Explorations
Giulia Rambelli

The Meaning of Constructions
Benoît Leclercq and Cameron Morin

Unrealized Arguments and the Grammar of Context
Rui P. Chaves, Paul Kay and Laura A. Michaelis

Multimodal Construction Grammar
Elisabeth Zima

Syntactic Variation from Individuals to Populations: Language as a Complex System
Jonathan Dunn

A full series listing is available at: www.cambridge.org/EICG

For EU product safety concerns, contact us at Calle de José Abascal, 56–1°, 28003 Madrid, Spain or eugpsr@cambridge.org.

www.ingramcontent.com/pod-product-compliance
Lightning Source LLC
LaVergne TN
LVHW021948060526
838200LV00043B/1959

* 9 7 8 1 0 0 9 4 2 0 3 0 3 *